THE

JESUS

EXPERIENCE

● YOU may not know Jesus yet. But he has always known and loved you. You are reading these lines now because he wants you to think about him.

● THE more you think about him, the more interesting he becomes for you. The more you experience him, the more interesting you become — for yourself.

● HE is your greatest and most loyal friend. May you find him in the pages of this book — and never lose him again!

Edward Carter sj

THE

JESUS

EXPERIENCE

ALBA BOOKS
DIV OF SOC OF ST PAUL CANFIELD OHIO 44406

IMPRIMI POTEST:

Daniel Flaherty, S.J.
Provincial
Chicago Province, Society of Jesus

NIHIL OBSTAT:

Edward Brueggeman, S.J.
Censor Deputatus

IMPRIMATUR:

Joseph Bernardin
Archbishop of Cincinnati

Library of Congress Catalog Card Number: 76-6701
ISBN   0 — 8189 — 1131 — X
© Copyright 1976 by Alba House Communications, Canfield, Ohio 44406

Printed in the United States of America

THE AUTHOR

Fr. Edward Carter is Professor of Theology at Xavier University, Cincinnati, Ohio, and is known across the country for his talks and retreats to priests, religious and laity. He has written nine books and innumerable articles. Four of his works have been Book Club selections and others have been translated into Italian, Portuguese and Polish.

Books by Edward Carter:

Everyday and Its Possibilities
The Jesus Experience
Jesus, I Want to Talk with You
Now Is the Time
Prayer Is Love
Response in Christ
The Spirit Is Present
Spirituality for Modern Man

Are there ALBA BOOKS titles you want but cannot find in your local stores? Simply send name of book and retail price plus 30¢ to cover mailing and handling costs to: ALBA BOOKS, Canfield, Ohio, 44406.

Table of Contents

1.	The Jesus Experience	1
2.	The Joy and Pain of Love	9
3.	To Be Free	17
4.	Involvement with the City of Man	21
5.	And There Is Loneliness	25
6.	Dimensions of Community	29
7.	Encounter with Others	33
8.	Suffering	39
9.	The Challenge of Becoming	43
10.	Prayer Encounter	47
11.	Humility Is a Mighty Virtue	57
12.	Maintaining Perspective	61
13.	Inconsistencies	65
14.	On Being Relevant	67
15.	Reconciliation	69
16.	The Call To Be Joyful	73
17.	Escapism	75
18.	Seasons of Life	77

19. The Role of Patience	81
20. Limitations	83
21. The Power of Affirmation	85
22. Contemplative Awareness	87
23. Touches of Goodness	91
24. Memories	95
25. The Thrust of Hope	97
26. Searching	99
27. Eucharist	101
28. Experiencing God	103

Permission to reproduce material from their publications has been courteously granted by Abingdon Press, Dimension Books, Doubleday & Co., Helicon Press, Herder & Herder, Pflaum Press, J. B. Lippincott Co., Paulist-Newman Press, Sheed & Ward, Templegate Publishers and the Editor of The Liguorian.

Details of these publications are grouped together at end.

Excerpts from homilies by the author, published in HOMILETIC AND PASTORAL REVIEW, February 1976, are reproduced by permission.

Excerpts from THE NEW AMERICAN BIBLE © are used by permission of the Confraternity of Christian Doctrine, copyright owner.

Photos: P. 8, Paul R. Schell, Youngstown; P. 46, THE GREATEST STORY EVER TOLD; P. 56, Standard Oil Co.; P. 60 and P. 64, W. Forres Stewart; back cover, THE GOSPEL ACCORDING TO ST. MATTHEW.

PREFACE

All authentically human activities and experiences are meant to be expressions of our Christian existence. Whether we work or play, suffer or rejoice, experience the glow of success or the sting of failure —— we are meant to be living in Christ Jesus.

This book of reflections is based on this very fact — that the Christian lives in, with, and through Jesus. We are truly called to live the Jesus experience. The following pages offer one person's thoughts of various ways in which we live the human condition in union with Jesus. These reflections, then, are reflections on being Christian.

These thoughts can be variously used. They may simply provide a form of spiritual reading. Or they may serve as an aid for prayer and reflection. The reader, of course, will think of topics which I have not treated, or will think of different ways of treating the themes I have reflected on. The important thing is that each of us takes the time to reflect on how much Jesus loves us, and on all the different ways he wants us to experience life in union with him.

I wish to take this opportunity to thank Father Edward Brueggeman, S.J., and all others for their kind assistance. I owe special gratitude to Joan Guntzelman for her careful typing of the manuscript and for her helpful advice.

Edward Carter, S.J.
Xavier University
Cincinnati, Ohio

THE THREE WAYS

There are three basic ways in which we can answer the call of Jesus: we can listen to his invitation, and, in the mystery of our free will, refuse him, choosing rather our own ill-conceived plan for human existence; we can respond, but with limited enthusiasm and commitment, and our lives are blemished with a terrible mediocrity; we can respond, telling Jesus that, despite our weakness, there is nothing we wish to hold back.

1. *The Jesus Experience*

● Jesus invites us but he does not coerce. He offers a religion which expands the person, not one which morbidly constricts. He offers us the fullness of life, but he does not deceitfully say there will be no suffering involved. He wants us to live the human condition as his intimate friends — he invites us to live the Jesus experience.

● Living the Jesus experience is not meant to be a part-time occupation: "The fact is that whether you eat or drink — whatever you do — you should do all for the glory of God" (1 Cor. 10:31).

● To live the grace-life is to live the Christ-life. As Rahner states: "... we only have a Christian understanding of grace when it is conceived of not only in the most metaphysical way possible, as a divinization, but rather as assimilation to Christ. And the existential transposition of this is the following of Christ..." [1]

- To follow Jesus is not to lessen our being authentically human. Rather, to follow Jesus allows us to be more human — in Christ we have a deepened, graced capacity to live the really real, the authentically human.

- Jesus has died and risen. We have been baptized into his death and resurrection. Each Christian act is characterized by this Christian pattern. Whether we work or play, experience success or failure, are admired or ridiculed, taste ecstatic happiness or feel overwhelmed with the cruel and evil aspect of human existence — we are dying and rising with Jesus.

- Why should the world's harsh dimension blind the Christian concerning its basic truth, goodness, and beauty? For to travel life's journey with this friend Jesus is to share his vision, a vision which permits us to see the world's Christic image, which nothing, absolutely nothing, can destroy.

- Jesus loves us. Allowing the realization of this simple yet awesome truth to guide our being and our becoming is to be fully Christian.

- "The rather simple, straightforward, and shocking message which Jesus came to bring was an attempt to redirect the course of human history, to change the style of human behavior and transform the nature of human relationships, and to reorder human life." [2]

● The committed Christian must consistently ask, "Is Jesus really the focal point of my existence?"

● "How many Christians really listen to Jesus' message?" is a question I can ask but cannot answer. "How do *I* listen to Jesus' message?" is a question that I should ask and can answer.

● Jesus gathers up what would otherwise be the all-too-fragmented pieces of my existence — the joy and the pain, the laughter and the tears, the success and the failure — and molds these into a Christic unity.

● "He wanted to be a man in times of triumph and torment, among the fawning palms, the sobs in the garden, the cries of the crucifixion. But for a longer period he wanted to live a commonplace life so as to be our companion in the mediocrity of ordinary working days; so that, in every solitary and insignificant moment, in every wretched and unwanted occupation, in the hidden places of our greyest hours, we would know that he had passed here too; he too loved the knife and the lantern, the chair and the fly, summer and winter." [3]

● We are an enigma to ourselves when we seek happiness apart from the way of Jesus, knowing within the depths of our being that following such a path leads to hideous frustration.

- This or that person may not realize our present suffering. But Jesus knows — and he cares.

- The tender and reassuring touch of Jesus — we can experience this in all sorts of situations, and, sometimes, when we least expect it.

- "The big problem that confronts Christianity is not Christ's enemies. Persecution has never done much harm to the inner life of the Church as such. The real religious problem exists in the souls of those who in their hearts believe in God, and who recognize their obligation to love Him and serve Him — yet do not!" [4]

- Jesus chose to lead much of his life in an obscure and disparaged place called Nazareth. This tells us something, if we have ears with which to hear.

- The Jesus experience is fundamentally an experience of love. To further fathom and assimilate the mystery of the Incarnation, we must love, and be open to love.

- It is sad, but true, that many Christians seem to have little or no desire for learning more about Jesus. Yet they eagerly pursue further knowledge concerning all sorts of other things.

- "Come to me, all you who are weary and find life burdensome, and I will refresh you. Take my yoke upon your shoulders and learn from me, for I am gentle and humble of heart. Your souls will find rest, for my yoke is easy and my burden light" (Mt. 11:28-30).

- Jesus loved us and poured himself out for us until there was no more to give. This is the poignant beauty of his life.

- How can we refuse to love anybody, since all have been touched by Jesus' redemptive blood? The Jesus experience excludes no one.

- We can be tempted to think the way of Jesus is all too difficult. Yet our faith-vision reminds us, "From this time on, many of his disciples broke away and would not remain in his company any longer. Jesus then said to the Twelve, 'Do you want to leave me too?' Simon Peter answered him, 'Lord, to whom shall we go? You have the words of eternal life'" (Jn. 6:66-68).

- As we are drawn into the Jesus experience by God's merciful love, we are graced with a new vision. St. Augustine says: "He came, clothed in healing human clay, to cure our interior eyes which our outer earthy vesture had blinded, so that, with soundness of vision restored, we who had before been darkness might become a shining light in the Lord, and so that the Light might no longer shine in darkness but might be clearly envisaged by those perceiving it." [5]

- The Son's descent into human flesh has given birth to a milieu of love. We can either harden ourselves to this love's influence, or open up to its power of marvelous expansiveness.

- Jesus has looked at me, and his gaze was so attractive. Jesus has reached out and touched me, and this made all the difference.

- Jesus has left his indelible imprint upon the human condition by the way he laughed and cried, worked and played, suffered and rejoiced — and above all by the way he loved.

- We at times refuse the voice of Jesus — we do not respond, we do not give, we do not grow in selflessness, we simply do not live as we should. Is it because of fear, or laziness, or sensuality, or pride, or rationalization? Whatever the cause, it is never a good excuse.

- The acclaimed and the unnoticed, the lettered and the unlettered, the old and the young, the laborer and the scholar, the comely and the homely — people from all classes and situations have, over the ages, been inspired by the one called Jesus.

- Our own enthusiasm for Jesus can be aided by recalling the fervor of those who have preceded us in the cause of Christ. One of these, St. Ignatius of Antioch, wrote during the first ages of Christianity: "Neither the kingdoms of this world nor the bounds of the universe can have any use for me. I would rather die for Jesus Christ than rule the last reaches of the earth. My search is for Him who died for us; my love is for Him who rose for our salvation." [6]

● Jesus knows our weakness far better than we ourselves. Still, he expects great things of us. Indeed, he has left us a unique formula, one that moreover seems strange to the unbelieving: our weakness plus his strength can accomplish the marvelous, whether the marvelous be hidden or well-known, whether it appear to others as extremely important or seemingly insignificant.

● The fact that children loved to be close to Jesus tells us so much about him.

● Jesus loved nature, and its beauty reminded him of his Father: "Learn a lesson from the way the wild flowers grow. They do not work; they do not spin. Yet I assure you, not even Solomon in all his splendor was arrayed like one of these. If God can clothe in such splendor the grass of the field, which blooms today and is thrown on the fire tomorrow, will he not provide much more for you, O weak in faith!" (Mt. 6:28-30).

If our laziness or insensitivity does not blind us regarding nature's beauty, it can remind us, too, of the Father.

● His enemies have tried to stamp out the memory of the man Jesus. Yet he and his message are still vitally present, so much so that for countless persons life is meaningless without him.

2. The Joy and Pain of Love

● Love is what makes the world go around, so the saying goes. To love and be loved sustains a person, promotes his growth, and encourages him even when the harsh and cruel aspect of the human condition is overwhelmingly felt.

● There is no danger in loving another too much. There is danger in loving another non-authentically — authentic love can become, at least partially, non-love. To recognize the difference between love and non-love can present a difficulty; the difficulty, however, does not remove the necessity of striving to discern the difference.

● To allow others to love us is itself a way of loving them. To be open appropriately to another's love affords that person an opportunity to grow through the act of loving. This, then, is a true act of love — for to love another is to assist that person in being and becoming what God destines him to be.

- As love grows and matures, it moves toward non-possessiveness. Mature love realizes that others should appropriately be allowed to share the beauty and the goodness of the loved one. Mature love realizes that others should benefit from the presence and the talents of the loved one. Mature love realizes all this — not, however, without at least some occasional pain. Diminishing and controlling the aspect of selfish possessiveness can cause suffering. The suffering, however, is less than that caused by our immature clinging to the loved one.

Authentic love also moves toward non-possessiveness because it realizes the loved one needs the freedom to encounter others, to be with others, to serve others. If I truly love another, I recognize that the loved one grows not only through encounter with myself, but through interaction with myriad types of persons in a variety of circumstances and situations.

- Jesus has told us to make love our main concern. Is it not strange that we Christians, who call ourselves his followers, can at times so easily allow other concerns to dominate our consciousness?

- When loving becomes difficult and painful, there is a temptation to turn in a direction which deceptively appears to be free of pain and trauma. Pursuing such a path can relieve one of love's suffering. Yet it is a dead-end street where one painfully suffocates in selfish self-enclosedness.

- To love opens oneself up to the possibility of being hurt by those one loves. However, not to love permits a person to be hurt by himself. For not to love is inflicting upon oneself the hurt of stunted growth.

- "Now I will show you the way which surpasses all the others. If I speak with human tongues and angelic as well, but do not have love, I am a noisy gong, a clanging cymbal. If I have the gift of prophecy and, with full knowledge, comprehend all mysteries, if I have faith great enough to move mountains, but have not love, I am nothing. If I give everything I have to feed the poor and hand over my body to be burned, but have not love, I gain nothing" (I Cor. 13:1-3).

- Love refuses to be jealous. Love rejoices over the good in others, encourages their efforts, acclaims their success.

- Although love must be firm when necessary, it is also gentle. Love does not further crush the bruised personality, but helps the other to heal and grow through tenderness and affirmation.

- The bloated stomachs of starving children, the tragedies of broken homes, the rat-infested ghettoes, the drug scene with its dreadful number of ruined lives, city streets engraved with an alarmingly growing list of murders, rapes, and muggings — when love sees all this, it weeps. Love not only weeps, however. It also acts.

● Jesus loves us. Why do we at times find it so difficult to love ourselves? Jesus sees our limitations, but also our capacity for achieving good. Why do we at times become depressed at what we are not, rather than being buoyed up at what God helps us to be?

● "I could not even begin to count the men and women whom I have met in my work who testify, with great sadness, that their formation/education both at home and at school was almost completely in terms of *achievement*, of doing, of performing according to standards, of accomplishing certain narrow goals — but hardly ever in terms of being, of growing, of loving."[1]

● Love is sensitive; it is delicately aware of the loved one's need. Moreover, love's sensitivity is blended with a strength and durability which allows it to endure pain, hardship, and difficulty for the beloved.

Love is sensitive not only regarding those few especially loved in close personal encounter. Love is sensitive also regarding all others, especially the poor and underprivileged, and those whom the world passes by as unimportant, the sick and the lame also, and likewise all those who seem especially weighed down with the burden of life.

● When love fails, it does not remain mired in discouragement. It resolves to learn from past mistakes and henceforth to love more selflessly, more deeply, more tenderly.

● Why are we sometimes afraid of God's love? We shy away from the white heat of his love, foolishly thinking he will ask too much of us. When has he ever asked something too difficult? When has he ever asked anything without giving us abundant grace to accomplish his desire? When has he ever asked that which has not brought us closer to him and enhanced our happiness?

● The unitive knowledge of God in love is not a knowledge of an object by a subject, but a far different and transcendent kind of knowledge in which the created 'self' which we are seems to disappear in God and to know him alone. In passive purification then the self undergoes a kind of emptying and an apparent destruction, until, reduced to emptiness, it no longer knows itself apart from God." [2]

● Sufferings are diminished when shared with a loved one; joys, on the other hand, are increased.

● One of love's crosses is that for the most part it must serve in such an uneventful way. Love rarely has the opportunity to manifest itself through heroic deeds. It's heroism usually must consist in performing the prosaic with magnanimity.

● Loving God occasions a measure of suffering — is there any loving which does not? Not loving God, however, brings about a much greater share of pain.

- To love God is to exercise our greatest privilege.

- He was consistently motivated by love. In the end he was literally consumed by love, for it led him to a place called Calvary. He was nailed to a cross, and raised up midst the laughter and ridicule of enemies. He hung there, bruised and beaten, his young, manly body smeared with blood. There was the flush of fever mixed with the chill of approaching death. The greatest physical suffering was surpassed only by an unfathomable anguish of spirit. It was a terrible scene, yet one permeated with a haunting beauty which sprang forth from the love of his heart. His crucified figure, silhouetted against a darkening sky, is the everlasting reminder that to live is to love.

- You have to help me to love; I must also help you.

- We are great because of what we are, and we are to the extent that we love.

- God incarnated his love for us through the enfleshment of his Son Jesus. We must also incarnate —visibly express — our love for others. Man is not a pure spirit, but spirit incarnated. Man has, therefore, an innate desire to express and experience love in the external, visible order — through the understanding word, the kind and welcoming smile, the tender touch, the maternal stroke of a child's hand, the kiss and embrace which say, "I love you."

- When another loves me, I feel secure — secure enough to become more myself. In the security of the other's love, there is no need to present a facade. The other's love encourages me to become more what God destines me to be.

- As I grow in authentic love for one; I simultaneously grow in my capacity to love all others more deeply.

- Love can cause one to weep. Sometimes the tears are caused by joy; at other times, by pain.

- Love looks first to see others' good points, while realistically admitting their imperfections. Love helps others to grow by affirming their capacity for good rather than by dwelling on what should not be.

- Love helps one to be enthusiastic about life, sometimes ecstatically so, more often quietly so.

- Two united in love encounter together the varied experiences of life within the human condition. Together they know laughter and tears, encounter success and failure, feel intense joy and anguished suffering. Throughout these myriad and diverse experiences, however, there is a constant which makes dissimilar experiences in one sense similar. This constant is their love for each other.

● St. Paul experienced love thrusting deeply to his innermost being: "I have been crucified with Christ, and the life I live now is not my own; Christ is living in me. I still live my own human life, but it is a life of faith in the Son of God, who loved me and gave himself for me" (Gal. 2:19:20).

● The path of life now stretches out straight, now twists and turns, now descends into the valley, now ascends to the hilltop where the horizon can be clearly seen. And all along, love is meant to be there, inspiring us to be and to become for God and our fellowmen.

3. To Be Free

● The more we give our freedom to Jesus, the freer we become.

● We are given freedom to attain the fullness of existence. When we abuse freedom, then, we are frustrating our potential for life.

● A good law, while in one sense restrictive, is fundamentally liberative. It channels our freedom in a Christic direction, thus liberating us from the morbid constrictions of a path opposed to God.

● Van Zeller says: "It is a Christian paradox that we free ourselves from the burden of the law only when we have accepted the burden of the law."[1]

● As we become more united to God in love, we grow in true liberty. For closer union with God means a greater actualization of our divinized, Christic selves, an actualization which includes a further assimilation of authentic freedom.

The Jesus Experience

● One of the greatest tyrannies is to be enslaved to selfish ego-centrism.

● Choosing forbidden pleasure deceitfully promises a kind of expansive, liberating experience. Such a choice, however, only contributes to the process of stifling self-enclosement — it is experiencing only oneself, rather than oneself in union with God through the proper use of freedom.

● "Creative freedom is not so much freedom from something as freedom for something, and in fact actually freedom to serve. The success of the freedom of the sons of God is their childlike service." [2]

● To exercise our freedom properly can at times occasion others feeling alienated from us for a variety of reasons. To violate our conscience in the incorrect use of freedom, however, contributes to the process of our feeling alienated from our true selves.

> "Jesus then went on to say to those Jews who believed in him:
> 'If you live according to my teaching, you are truly my disciples;
> then you will know the truth, and the truth will set you free.'" (Jn 8:31-32).

● Often growth in being Christic-free is relatively easy. Occasionally, however, escape from the shackles of our unfreedom comes only through a mighty effort.

● Jesus paid a great price to achieve our freedom. Do we dare squander it?

● Although those who are enslaved to the things of the world do indeed seem to have a love for it, in reality they do not authentically cherish the world. Their apparent love is actually a selfishness. Because of their enslavement to the world they are not free enough to contribute properly to its true progress.

● If we are free enough to give up something if God so asks, we are simultaneously free enough fully to enjoy that something as God allows. Authentic joy and happiness emanate from the use of creatures only when we possess the freedom to relate to these according to God's will.

● "When you were slaves of sin, you had freedom from justice. What benefit did you then enjoy? Things you are now ashamed of, all of them tending toward death. But now that you are freed from sin and have become slaves of God, your benefit is sanctification as you tend toward eternal life." (Rom 6:21-22).

● Sometimes we think we are ready to be completely generous with God — then he asks something we had least expected and our unfreedom refuses him. At other times we are surprised how generous our graced freedom renders us. On these occasions we are in awe that our response is seemingly of heroic proportions.

- Growth in docility to the Spirit requires a corresponding growth in the freedom Christ came to give. If we are not free enough, there are various possibilities which can occasion our refusing what the Spirit quietly asks of us.

- That which principally thrusts us toward greater freedom is love — love of God and man in Christ. Love, despite what suffering may be involved, impels us to become more free so that we can more fully make the on-going gift of self which Christianity insistently demands.

4. Involvement with the City of Man

● Jesus, through his Incarnation, has drawn to himself not only man, but man's world as well: "Christ's work of redemption is directed both toward the salvation of men, as individuals, and at the renewal of the whole secular order."[1]

● The temporal order, then, belongs to Jesus. Are we not called, therefore, to love it, to promote its authentic growth, to help its Christic image shine forth more clearly?

● Men are variously influenced by temporal institutions — for example, by the world of politics, business, economics, culture, entertainment. To love our neighbor means, in part, to be seriously concerned in contributing to the proper shaping of these institutions — helping them better serve the temporal and eternal destinies of the human race.

- As the temporal order becomes more Christic, it simultaneously becomes more itself. Christ has assumed the temporal order, not to lessen its terrestrial value, but to increase it. The more the temporal is Christianized, however unobstrusively and hiddenly, the more truly liberated it becomes — the freer it becomes to develop its possibilities for serving the authentic needs of man.

- Since the world belongs to Christ, the Christian should feel at home in it, loving what is good, hating what is evil, laboring that all may be more in harmony with the priceless dignity of man.

- For the Christian, there can be no question whether or not he should be concerned with the secular order. Whether he be inner city worker or Trappist monk, the question is rather how God would have him implement this concern.

- "Creation was made subject to futility, not of its own accord but by him who once subjected it; yet not without hope, because the world itself will be freed from its slavery to corruption and share in the glorious freedom of the children of God. Yes, we know that all creation groans and is in agony even until now." (Rom 8:20-22).

- The temporal is the milieu in which the eternal is shaped — our eternities will evolve from our encounter with the varied dimensions comprising the human condition, a spectrum made up of experiences ranging from agony to ecstasy.

● There is so much about the temporal order we prefer not always to think about — because such a recollection disturbs our complacency, and, because of its call to action, threatens our leisure and our comfort.

● The child, a member of the world's disinherited, looks into our eyes. In his own we see sadness and despair, so inappropriate for his tender age, yet unmistakably put there by that in the world which should not be.

● What is gained by our fanciful flight from the authentic demands of earthly life? Surely not a further stage in the pilgrimage of true becoming.

● Some work amid circumstances charged with potential explosiveness; some work within the confines of a clean and quiet office. Some perform, claiming the attention of the public eye; others labor in hidden ordinariness. Some must fight the bordeom which routine work tends to generate; others must maintain high-level awareness amid the dangerous novelty of high-risk occupations. However, whatever be the task and its circumstances in the city of man, the imperative is the same for all: to be where God wants us.

● All types contribute variously to the shaping of a better world: the young, their enthusiasm; the old, their mellowed wisdom; the conservative, their concern for timeless values; the progressive, their reaching out for that which has not yet been attained.

- Jesus objectively redeemed us by his immersion into the human condition. We are subjectively redeemed through a similar immersion.

- On certain days we see the sky — clear blue, all blue, fresh blue — glistening with the rays of a golden sun. And beneath the blue and golden sky there stretches forth a segment of the secular city — the city of man and the city of God. As the sky has its beauty from above, so the secular city has its beauty from below, a beauty partially created by the goodness of man, yet a beauty scarred with a blemish caused by the evil of man. We pray that the beauty may increase and the blemish decrease — and we pledge our efforts to help this be so.

5. And There Is Loneliness

● There is that loneliness in our lives which need not be — a loneliness which can be alleviated by our properly relating to God and to others. There is also a loneliness which should be, a loneliness rooted in our existential condition as pilgrims — persons still longingly reaching out for that complete fulfillment, that absolute eradication of all loneliness, a condition reserved for the bliss of eternal life.

● "We ignore what we already know with a deep-seated intuitive knowledge — that no love or friendship, no intimate embrace or tender kiss, no community, commune or collective, no man or woman, will ever be able to satisfy our desire to be released from our lonely condition."[1]

● Failure can give birth to loneliness — but so also can success.

- Crowded apartment buildings, crowded places of amusement, crowded churches, crowded city streets, crowded airplanes and subways — in the midst of all this he still is lonely, a vivid example that merely being surrounded by people does not assuage the heart's loneliness. Rather it is being able to relate properly to others which helps alleviate this pain.

- It is time to decide, and despite all the advice and support we have received from others, we know that now the decision is ours alone. And we experience the loneliness of this condition.

- Loving and being loved can occasion loneliness. Not loving and not being loved also promotes loneliness. We all know which loneliness we prefer.

- It is natural to experience loneliness when a deeply loved one is far away. Yet there is another love-loneliness possible even when the beloved is physically very close.

- Encountering properly the loneliness of the human condition contributes to the process of maturing self-expansiveness. Rebelling childishly against this loneliness contributes to the process of self-enclosedness — a state which intensifies one's pain.

- We have all felt a particularly disturbing kind of loneliness — being so much misunderstood by those we so much love.

● Made orphan by the tragedy of war, the child cries out with an anguished and confused loneliness, a loneliness caused by forces he in no way understands, yet which have so pitilessly conditioned his life.

● Some are lonely because they have not yet found God, and their loneliness is bitter; others are lonely because they have found God, but long for a still closer union, and their loneliness is sweet.

● There is a vast difference between being lonely and being alone — although, granted, we can be very lonely on a particular occasion of being alone. Yet one can also be very much alone while simultaneously being very much not lonely.

● Feeling ostracized because we remain loyal to Spirit-inspired ideals can occasion a sensation of loneliness, yet it is a loneliness which in turn occasions an experience of an inner glow and peace emanating from the realization that we have been true to our Christic selves.

● Experiencing loneliness because one refuses to go out to others is a self-inflicted pain of enormously senseless proportions.

● Rejected by his beloved Jewish people, betrayed by Judas, denied by Peter, deserted by his disciples, he hung upon a cross. And the loneliness which pierced his magnanimous heart left a far greater wound than did the soldier's lance.

- One of the most tragic forms of loneliness is to be alienated from one's true self.

- Industrialized man can experience considerable difficulty identifying with his work. Scientific sophistication can produce a subtle barrier between the worker and his production with a consequent experience of work alienation or loneliness — unless one strives to pierce this barrier with a sense of personal uniqueness which assures a creative touch that no technology can destroy.

- If not all loneliness is to be removed during our earthly sojourn, there is, nonetheless, that type or degree which should not be. The radical solution in combating such loneliness is to walk in the presence of the Lord himself:

> The Lord is my shepherd; I shall not want.
> In verdant pastures he gives me repose;
> Besides restful waters he leads me; he refreshes my soul.
> He guides me in right paths for his name's sake.
> Even though I walk in the dark valley
> I fear no evil; for you are at my side
> With your rod and your staff that give me courage (Ps. 23. 1-4).

6. Dimensions of Community

● "There are, indeed, many different members, but one body. The eye cannot say to the hand, 'I do not need you,' any more than the head can say to the feet, 'I do not need you.' Even those members of the body which seem less important are in fact indispensable." (1 Cor 12: 20-22).

● I need you, you need me. Why at times do we pretend that it is otherwise?

● John Donne, far back in the seventeenth century, wrote these perennially applicable words: "No man is an island, entire of itselfe; every man is a piece of the *continent*, a part of the maine." [1]

● To expect the community which is the Church to be without sins and blemishes is to demand too much. On the other hand, to want the Church humbly to labor at a vigorous on-going conversion is to desire what the Spirit himself wishes.

- Any form of Christian community must gaze inward upon itself — in order to maintain and promote Spirit-inspired vitality. But if there is not a self-transcendence involved — a loving and concerned gaze outward toward the entire human family — then there is something tragically lacking.

- "There are, there were, and there will be weaknesses in the Church. What should be the response of a Christian? It cannot be anything else than the Christian response that is compassion. Bitter criticism and aggressive accusation do not heal wounds. If anything, they aggravate the condition of the sick. Besides, those attitudes hardly proceed from faith, hope and love." [2]

- The human family's sinfulness is abundantly manifest. But to concentrate on this rather than on man's goodness is to be afflicted with an unchristian pessimism.

- The little black boy and the little white boy hug each other in playful glee. How often little children can teach us — if we're not too stubborn and supercilious to listen.

- "The Church is in the first instance a sign. It must signify in a historically tangible form the redeeming grace of Christ. It signifies that grace as relevantly given to men of every age, race, kind, and condition. Hence the Church must incarnate itself in every human culture." [3]

- God has created each person marvelously unique. He has also made man a social being; hence each one's uniqueness is meant to unfold within the framework of community.

- Community is often built through pain-demanding and time-demanding effort. How quickly, though, one can harm community through the uncharitable, cutting, and divisive word.

- To walk the path of life hand in hand with my brother is Spirit-inspired wisdom. To want to walk alone is childish and pain-inflicting folly.

- Some are guilty because they unjustly use the structures and institutions of society variously to harm their fellowmen; others are guilty because they neglect their responsibility to aid in reforming and strengthening these same social structures.

- Do I sincerely rejoice in the good others do? If not, why not? Community thrives on such rejoicing.

- "The theologian is aware that this *inescapable responsibility for oneself*, which Christianity proclaims, must take the shape of self-forgetfulness in the love of one's fellows, or else it becomes the hell of one's own egoistic isolation." [4]

- The Christian community is intended to be a terrestrial reflection of that ultimate and perfect community — the Trinitarian life of Father, Son, and Holy Spirit.

- "In the name of the encouragement you owe me in Christ, in the name of the solace that love can give, of fellowship in spirit, compassion, and pity, I beg you: make my joy complete by your unanimity, possessing the one love, united in spirit and ideals. Never act out of rivalry or conceit; rather, let all parties think humbly of others as superior to themselves, each of you looking to others' interests rather than his own" (Phil. 2:1-4).

- Needlessly to hurt another is simultaneously to hurt myself.

7. Encounter with Others

● There are those who seek to encounter God while lacking a proper concern for their neighbor. There are those who reach out to touch their brothers while refusing God his due. Both classes are following a road paved with frustration.

● Love then, consists in this:
not that we have loved God,
but that he has loved us
and has sent his Son as an offering for
      our sins.

Beloved,
if God has loved us so,
we must have the same love for one
      another.

(1 Jn. 4:10:11).

● Manipulating others to satisfy our own needs is not the rarest of temptations.

- Feelings generated by encounter with others can run the gamut from excruciating pain to ecstatic happiness.

- At times we must flee others in order to be more authentically present to them. Without prayerful solitude we will not love them as we should.

- Each individual is a marvelous uniqueness created by God. To be aware of this wonder is to respect the priceless dignity of the other.

- "Repeatedly I have found, to my astonishment, that the feelings which have seemed to me most private, most personal, and therefore the feelings I least expect to be understood by others, when clearly expressed resonate deeply and consistently with their own experience. This has led me to believe that what I experience in the most unique and personal way, if brought to clear expression, is precisely what others are most deeply experiencing in analogous ways."[1]

- Others can tell me things about myself which are very evident to them, yet almost beyond my own awareness.

- If we do not believe in the basic goodness of others, we do not believe in ourselves.

- If we dwell more on what is wrong about others rather than what is right, this tells us that something is wrong about ourselves.

- To think I have no need of others is a sign I need them very much.

- He heard the anguished cry of his brother, otherwise named everyman. He refused to listen. The cry came again, and then again. He finally sought out his brother. He found him — and simultaneously found himself.

- There should be, of course, a basic and rather thorough openness between those engaged in close encounter. Yet we must beware of thinking that all should be revealed. There is an area of one's being meant to be clothed in mystery.

- "Aren't the many feelings of sadness, heaviness of heart and even dark despair, often intimately connected with the exaggerated seriousness with which we have clothed the people we know, the ideas to which we are exposed and the events we are part of? This lack of distance, which excludes the humor in life, can create a suffocating depression which prevents us from lifting our heads above the horizon of our own limited existence." [2]

- If we are too much filled with our own ideas about things, there is little room for proper openness to the views of others.

- We must not think that the more time we spend with a loved one the better. At times there must be various interludes of non-togetherness. Have you noticed that such episodes of separation tend to deepen our appreciation of the other's goodness and attractiveness?

- He who does not wish to share himself with others actually has very little to share.

- The more we encounter our own authentic, Christic selves, the more capable we become of authentically encountering others.

- When we irresponsibly flee Spirit-inspired encounter with others in order to avoid pain, we encounter our own ugliness — and this is the greater suffering.

- Unhealthy competitiveness, a drive so prevalent in so many areas of contemporary society, can produce its own rewards. Yet these are rewards just as unhealthy as their source, since they add to the sickness of their bearers, the sickness being a further separation from the neighbor.

- When we are aware of our poverty — of our spiritual need — we have the potential to be enriched by others.

- Not to love others is to not love ourselves.

- In God's providence, we are meant to develop a closeness to certain individuals and they to us. It is, however, not a suffocating kind of closeness, but one which allows a freer breathing emanating from expanded growth, a growth facilitated by mutual sharing.

● Have you ever walked along a crowded city street, and felt a oneness with the people whom you did not know, had never seen, and most probably would never see again? These are graced moments of brotherly awareness. We should thank God for them, and build upon them, as we strive for a deepened consciousness of how Jesus has extended his arms on the cross in order to draw all together in a precious closeness.

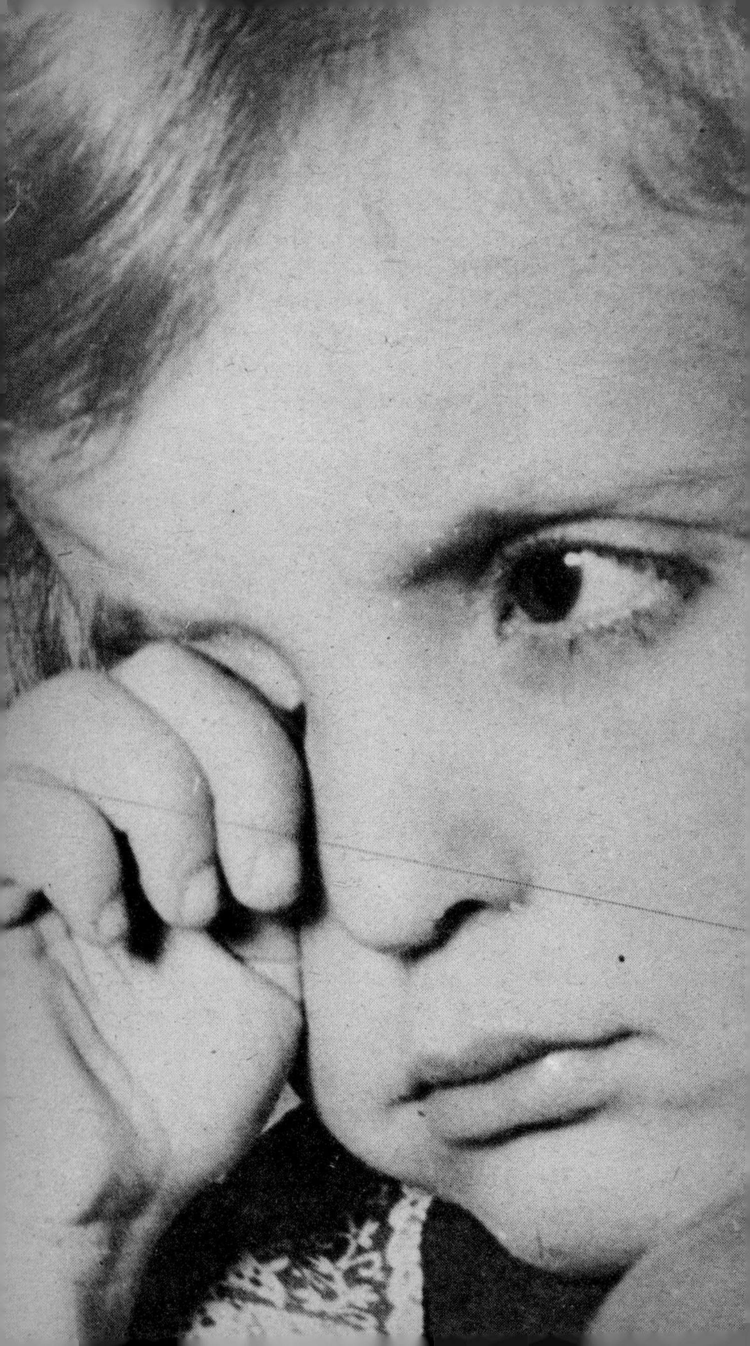

8. Suffering

- Though he was harshly treated, he submitted
  and opened not his mouth;
  Like a lamb led to the slaughter
  or a sheep before the shearer,
  he was silent and opened not his mouth. (Is. 53:7).

- The great tragedy concerning human suffering is not that it is so abundantly present. The real tragedy is that apparently so much of it is wasted.

- Suffering can beautifully expand or bitterly constrict the personality. It is our choice which alternative prevails.

- "When we suffer and no longer know why, when we suffer without rejoicing, then we are outside of the genuine Christian experience." [1]

- A willingness to suffer for a cause must accompany any true commitment.

- A persistent suffering is the necessity of bearing with our limitations.

- The fear of suffering is, for some people, one of their greatest crosses.

- True love, in any of its forms, must be expressed and experienced against the background of the cross. Jesus has very poignantly and very vividly shown us this. Strange, then, that we seemingly can strive to develop another pattern of loving.

- That suffering which is presently the most necessary for us is the one we can most consistently refuse.

- Happiness cannot be achieved without a proper encounter with suffering. This is a basic premise of the Christian message. It would seem, then, that we would eagerly embrace the cross. And yet, how often is this the case?

- Being misunderstood by others precisely because we are striving to do God's will is a not uncommon suffering.

- To have to unavoidably hurt others can cause the sensitive person a suffering greater than the one he is inflicting.

● Being unloved by that individual whom a person deeply loves is one of the greatest pains which wound the human heart.

● To be forced to choose, in crucial situations, while being uncertain what to choose is an unusually penetrating kind of distress.

● There is a part of us which does not want to surrender to God. The struggle between the good self and the evil self produces an unique type of pain which is persistently present, often to a degree which is quite tolerable, but occasionally with an intensity that pierces very suddenly and very sharply.

● It is not those who suffer the most who are necessarily the holiest. We grow in holiness through suffering — whatever its degree — to the extent that we encounter it as God wills.

● The boredom which can grow out of daily routine, the frequent occasions which try one's patience, the lack of outsanding success in our work coupled with at least occasional failure, minor annoyances of various kinds, anxieties — these and other forms of the daily cross do not, taken separately, require a Christian response of heroic proportions. But in their cumulative effect over a long period of time, such occasions offer us the opportunity of becoming love-inspired Christians to an eminent degree.

- There is nothing in the Christian doctrine of the cross which says we cannot pray for relief from our sufferings.

- To want to flee suffering is an unchristian attitude. So also is the attempt to make suffering an end in itself. The Christ-event did not end on Calvary.

- "Jesus said to all: 'Whoever wishes to be my follower must deny his very self, take up his cross each day, and follow in my steps. Whoever would save his life will lose it, and whoever loses his life for my sake will save it'" (Lk. 9:23-24).

9. The Challenge of Becoming

● To rest content with the present state of our existence is to be satisfied with mediocrity.

● Reaching out for a further assimilation of the Gospel ideal should be for us a dynamic imperative.

● There are times when we fear the pain of becoming, refuse, and, consequently, illogically choose the greater pain of stunted growth.

● As was Abraham before us, so too are we called forth to become that which God further destines us to be: "The Lord said to Abram: 'Go forth from the land of your kinsfolk and from your father's house to a land that I will show you'" (Gen. 12:1).

● Some acquire only very limited growth over a span of many years. Others achieve a becoming of magnificent proportions within a much shorter duration.

- There are special persons in our lives who have helped us become in a special way — indeed, without them, we may not have become in certain ways at all.

- God can lead us forth to a further becoming which necessitates, according to certain aspects, a departure from our past pattern of being Christian. This does not mean that the previous way was not the right way; it simply means that God is introducing certain changes, changes which sometimes appeal to us, but at other times do not. The important thing, though, is to follow the lead of the Lord.

- We can be called to become in a way that previously did not seem to be our way. We have to be supple enough to adapt to the Spirit's invitation.

- To discern true becoming requires spiritual perceptiveness — for apparent progress may actually constitute retrogression, and seeming retrogression, authentic growth.

- The journey of true becoming is at certain points illumined with the brightest light; at other points it is enveloped in an awesome darkness.

- Establishing set ways of doing things certainly can be an aid in facilely discharging numerous daily duties. Yet we must be aware lest such a pattern destroy our capacity to be properly open to that which is new, different, or evolving.

● To become through the proper use of success is a much desired route. To grow through the proper confrontation with failure is a much less popular way — yet a way which must blend in with other avenues in the process of anyone's true becoming.

● Sometimes we help others become by being with them; at other times, by leaving them in solitude.

● Days of excitement and days of boredom, times of anguish and times of overwhelming joy, periods of demanding work and episodes of peaceful relaxation, experiences of being accepted mixed in with occasions of being rejected — these are all opportunities for further becoming, provided we follow the Spirit's lead.

● To want to become without the support of others is a way marked with certain — and senseless — failure.

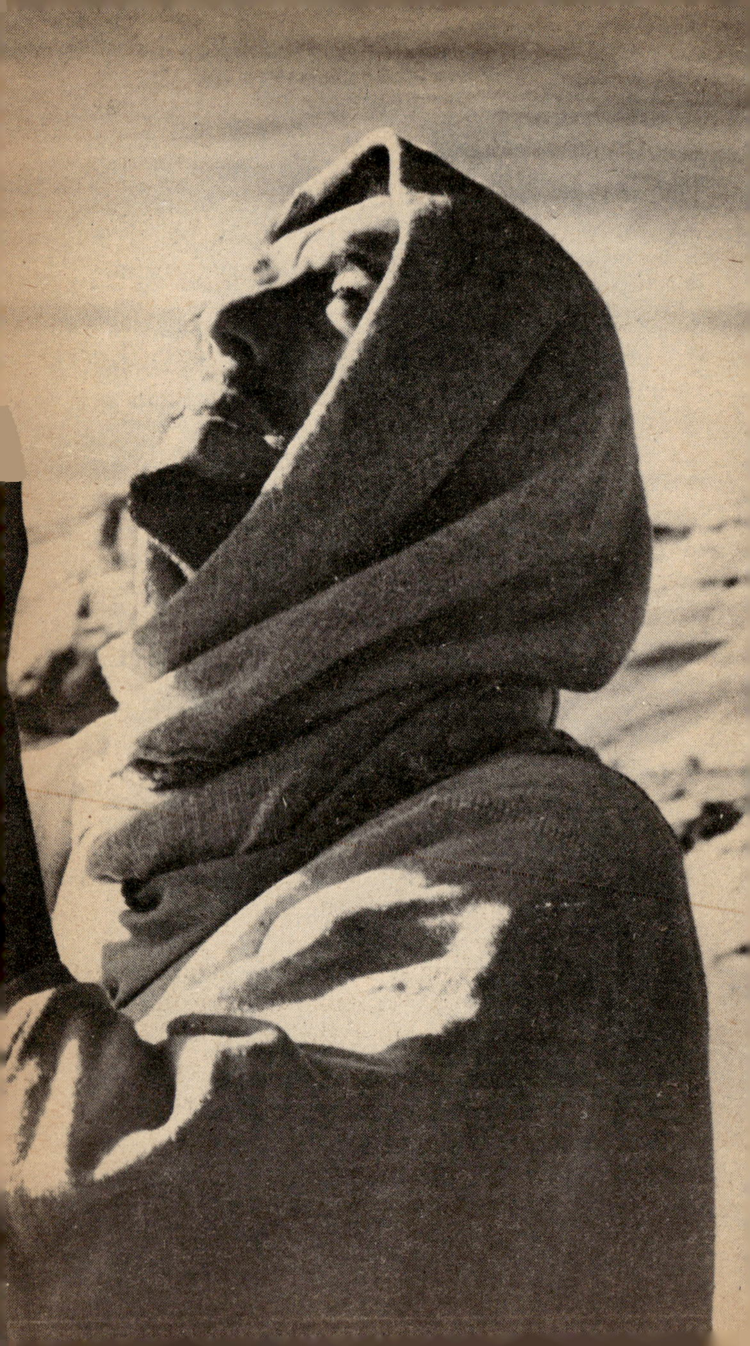

10. Prayer Encounter

● Prayer is a personal encounter. Prayer is a special awareness whereby I am conscious of God's presence to me and my presence to God.

The personal presence of prayer is permeated with love. Prayer is primarily a love. Prayer is my openness to the touch of God's love for me. Prayer is my response of love to God.

Prayer is also my love for God's creation — for people and all the rest. For in prayer my desire to relate to reality according to God's designs is deepened and refurbished.

● "Everyday life must train us to kindness, patience, peacefulness and understanding; to meekness and gentleness; to forbearance and endurance. In this way, everyday life becomes in itself *prayer*. All our interests are unified and exalted by the love of God; our scattered aims are given a specific direction towards God; our external life becomes the expression of our love of God." [1]

- Some say that prayer is a risk — that if we encounter God in prayer there is no assurance that what he asks of us will be to our liking. If prayer is a risk, it is a risk for happiness. When has God ever asked that which has not promoted our growth, our fulfillment, our happiness?

- In prayer God reveals himself to me. He also reveals me to myself. The light of prayer gradually cuts through the layers of the false self and penetrates to the real self, the Christic self. If I look at my authentic self, God will manifest to me what he destines me to be and what he destines me to become.

- Prayer helps purge away my selfishness and all else that should not be. This purgation occurs not without pain, but it is a life-giving pain, one that leads to a greater love, to a greater love-union with God and my fellowman.

- The light of prayer can at times allow us to see so clearly — so clearly that we wonder how we ever envisioned otherwise.

- When lethargy and boredom make my abilities and talents relatively dormant, I should pray. Prayer has a peculiar power to rekindle the fires of enthusiasm which seemed all but burnt out. Often the enthusiasm of prayer touches me in a quiet and low-keyed manner. But sometimes this enthusiasm shoots through me intensely, and I feel its penetrating and quickening force in every part of my being.

- Prayer makes us more sensitive regarding that which is not, yet should be, and that which is, but should not be.

- Prayer is both a means of nourishing our desire to know Jesus better and a source of satisfying that desire. In prayer we achieve an experiential knowledge of the Lord, a knowledge which fires our wills with a renewed love which prompts us to give Jesus all that we are and all that we have.

- What St. John of the Cross states concerning a special stage of infused contemplation, is proportionately true of any type of Christian prayer: "It remains to be said, then, that even though this happy night darkens the spirit, it does so only to impart light concerning all things; and even though it humbles a person and reveals his miseries, it does so only to exalt him; and even though it impoverishes and empties him ... it does so only that he may reach out divinely to the enjoyment of all earthly and heavenly things, with a general freedom of spirit in them all." [2] In other words, Christian prayer both purifies and unites — it occasions both death and resurrection.

- Although the Pentecostal or Charismatic movement is attracting more and more participants, it obviously is not for everyone. However, whether we ourselves are actively involved with Pentecostalism or not, we can profit from the movement. For example Charismatics remind us of a very important aspect of Christianity — that it is communal, that Christ has formed us into a People of God.

- Prayer is meant to expand us. Prayer is meant to deepen our relationship with God, with loved ones, with the entire human race. Prayer is meant to help release us from the suffocating confines of introverted selfishness. If a person prays and remains self-enclosed, something is remiss.

- We can say we will not pray today because we feel lazy, or tired, or because we're too busy, or because a particular problem is depressing us, or simply because we are not in a very religious mood. If we capitulate to this attitude, we are being extremely hard on prayer — demanding the perfect situation before we pray. Would we do *anything* in life if we awaited the ideal situation?

- Prayer is a factor in our controlling the temptation to flee painful and demanding reality. The light of prayer can help us see that to be mature Christians we must courageously face the painful aspect of life within the human condition. Prayer's light can convince us that to try to flee pain is to invite greater pain; for to flee life's painful dimension is to flee opportunities for growing, and this escape, consequently, leads us to experience the pain of truncated growth.

- Jesus was a busy man — yet he always found time to pray: "His reputation spread more and more, and great crowds gathered to hear him and to be cured of their maladies. He often retired to deserted places and prayed" (Lk. 5:15).

● Western culture renders easy our becoming "non-silent" people. There is the ready availability of television, and radio, and myriad other types of distractions which, even though not all involve sound as such, can destroy our inner silence. Such distractions can too much absorb our attention and thereby prevent us from entering into the inner self where lies a great source of our authentic vitality and personal integration. There is a time for everything, and, therefore, a proper time for television and radio and the rest. But there is also a time for the silence which promotes prayerful reflection and meditation.

We may be avoiding prayerful silence because we fear its truth — the truth about ourselves, our activities, our attitudes, about Jesus Himself. We may be fearful of the truth which prayerful silence whispers because of what that truth may demand. The truth, however, is meant to make us free. The more we live the truth, the more free and happy we become. The words of prayerful silence, then, are words of freedom, fulfillment, peace, and happiness.

● "Is my life really no more than a single short aspiration, and all my prayers just different formulations of it in human words? Is the eternal possession of You Your eternal answer to it? Is Your silence when I pray really a discourse filled with infinite promise, unimaginably more meaningful than any audible word You could speak to the limited understanding of my narrow heart, a word that would itself have to become as small and poor as I am?" [3]

● To expect prayer continually to give us an emotional high is to misjudge the purpose of prayer. Such erroneous expectations invite frustration and can easily lead to the abandonment of prayer. True, we should pray with our total being, emotions included. It is, then, a good to experience noticeably the movement of the emotions during prayer. But this emotional overtone is not essential, and, if absent, we should not think our time at prayer is squandered time. Prayer centers in the love activity of the will, and this love activity is by no means always accompanied by emotional consolation.

● Distractions can frequently occur in the life of prayer. Only when one enjoys higher mystical prayer are distractions totally absent, and apparently only a relatively few persons are graced with such prayer. Our attitude regarding distractions during prayer, then, should not be to expect a complete lack of distractions. Our attitude should rather be one which moves us to exert the quiet but firm effort necessary for the proper control of these distractions.

● Prayer offers us the opportunity to develop our sense of mystery and wonder. If we do not pray, much of life's beauty, and mystery, and wonderfulness can escape unnoticed.

In prayer we thank God for making us part of life's mystery. In prayer we gaze in wonder at the mystery of God's love for us. In prayer we feel secure in this intimate, tender, and personal love.

● During prayer we can encounter episodes during which little or nothing seems to be happening — and on such occasions we are tempted to think we are wasting time. If we aspire to a consistent prayer life, we must recognize and resist this temptation. We must adjust to this apparent uselessness of prayer. Notice we say *apparent* uselessness, for, if we are making reasonable efforts to pray well, these episodes are replete with their own fruitfulness, but a type of fruitfulness not easily recognized.

● The central emphasis of Zen-Buddhism is the quest of enlightenment. This enlightenment consists in seeing into what the Zen-Buddhist believes is true reality, the true nature of things. This enlightenment, sought in contemplation, is meant to guide the Buddhist in all aspects of living. This *satori*, or enlightenment, is a type of mystical vision of reality. Through *satori* the Zen-Buddhist does not so much see new things — he sees old things differently or in a new way. The Zen-Buddhist believes that through enlightenment he sees reality in a way he previously did not; now he believes he sees reality as it truly is.

● Our attempts at prayer must be built upon solid realism. We must approach the practice of prayer with a mature realization that prayer is a very rewarding experience, but that a consistent prayer-life is not always easily achieved.

- Seeking a more penetrating grasp of reality is also indigenous to Christian prayer. Through the light of prayer we can achieve a more perfect understanding of the ultimate reality who is God himself. Through the light of prayer we can also achieve a deepened insight into the reality which is the true self. In prayer we are meant to comprehend with a more finely-honed vision the reality of our lives. We are meant to grasp, with a realization made more penetrating through prayer's enlightenment, how the laughter and the tears, the work and the play, the pain, the suffering, the joy, and the happiness — how everything has a Christic unity, how in Christ the various pieces of our lives are meant to be gathered up and presented in a marvelous unity to the Father under the Spirit's guidance. Through prayer we likewise arrive at a deepened insight concerning the reality of our fellowmen — how each possesses a priceless dignity, how each has been redeemed by the blood of Jesus, how we should give ourselves to promote the temporal and eternal destinies of these — our sisters and our brothers.

The light of Christian prayer, then, gives us a deepened insight into all reality so that we see not a new reality, not a reality we were in no way previously aware of, but a reality that now appears differently because we now more maturely comprehend it. Prayer's insight, in turn, leads to prayer's love. Through prayer's enlightenment we see more penetratingly into what our relationship with God, neighbor, and all reality should be; through prayer's love we are led to live these relationships more profoundly.

● In prayer God embraces me with his love. The touch of this love is there, there always, although at times darkness and dryness may simultaneously be present.

● Contemplation in action, or a prayerful attitude which permeates our day, is obviously compatible with external activity —it helps orient all to God.

However, there also is a kind of prayer which demands stillness, a withdrawal from external activity. Unless we learn to be still so that we can pray and contemplate, then we will be less than we are meant to be. At the proper times we must learn to exchange the activity of external involvement for the activity of stillness which makes prayer possible.

● We can know all about various ways of praying and yet we will not pray unless we fundamentally desire to. If we really desire to pray, we will pray, one way or the other — and this is the important thing. This fundamental desire to pray consistently — which desire itself is something we should pray for — will see us through prayer's pilgrimage. If we really want to pray, we will, despite certain difficulties and even repugnances along the way. The deeper our desire for prayer, the easier prayer tends to become. The deeper our desire for prayer, the more we will look for ways of making prayer a greater part of our lives. The deeper our desire for prayer, the more we will thirst for God.

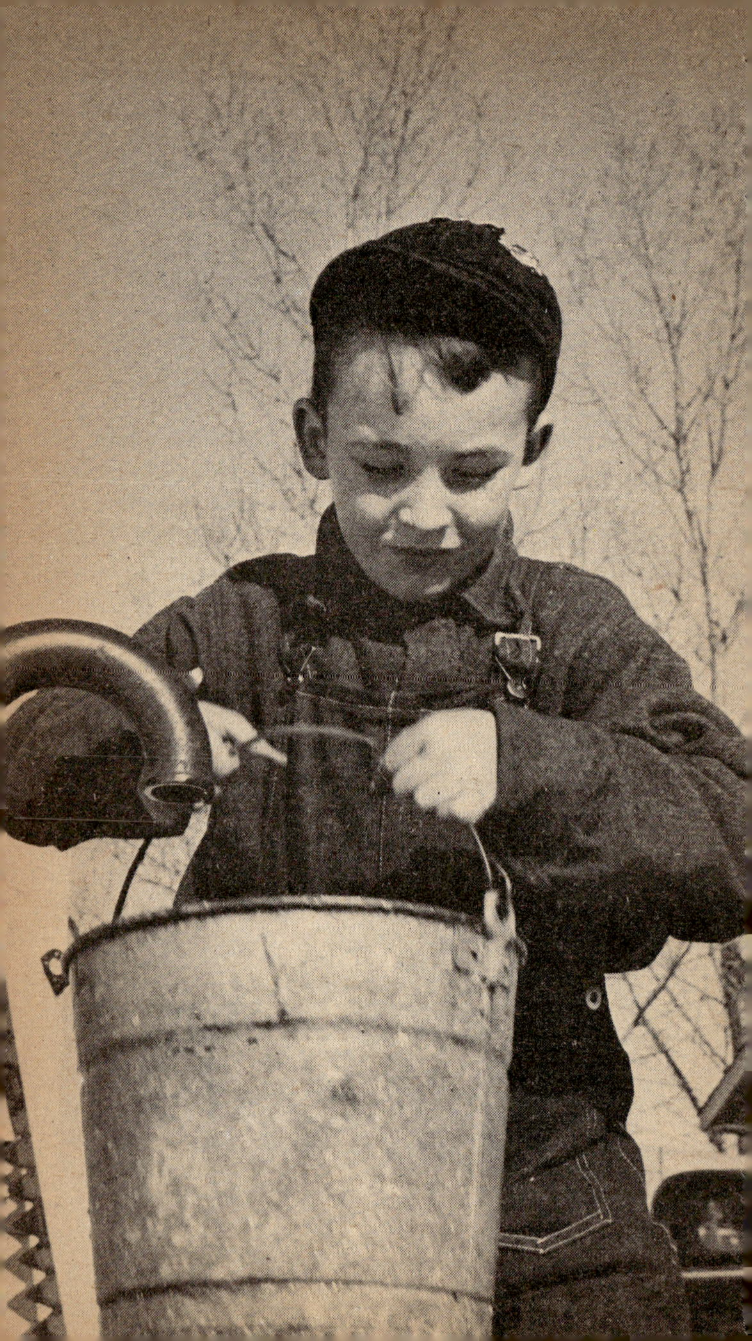

11. *Humility Is a Mighty Virtue*

● "Be humbled in the sight of the Lord and he will raise you on high" (Jas. 4:10).

● Humility is a mighty virtue becaues it empties us of proud egotism and makes room for the strength of the Lord.

● Humility is not a process of self-depreciation. Far from bidding us to deny our gifts and telling ourselves we are of little worth, humility directs our attention to all the gifts God has given us so that we may be properly thankful and aware of our responsibility to use our talents for the glory and service of the Lord.

● Humility also bids us to look at what is wrong about ourselves. If we are truly humble, such a process does not depress us, but fills us with the peace of the Lord as we determine to strive to become more what Jesus desires us to be.

- A humble person is a secure person. Humility focuses our attention not on ourselves but on God. Out of this God-centered mentality emanates a deepening realization that we are God's children and that he loves us mightily — and herein lies our deepest sense of feeling secure.

- Humility helps develop our openness and receptivity. A proud person is a self-enclosed individual, and is thereby hindered in being adorned with the beauty which comes from receptive encounter with God and one's fellowmen.

- Humility helps prevent us from being terribly mediocre — it prevents us from thinking that the present opportunity is unworthy of our talents, an attitude which tends to make our present service a half-hearted one.

- Jesus as man fully accepted his creaturehood. He accepted the full implications of being immersed within the human condition. In part this meant suffering, and ultimately suffering terribly, because of the evil in others. He did not flinch from this harsh dimension of human existence. He was truly humble.

- Humility does not make us distrust our own well-founded views and ideas about things. It does, however, allow us to realize how much we can learn about God's truth as it is prismed in so many different ways through the uniqueness of various individuals.

● Humility helps preserve us from that awful enslavement which is the constant desire to be praised and acclaimed by others.

● A proud person tends to complain that others do not give him his due. A humble person tends to be in awe at the goodness others lavish upon him.

● "Take my yoke upon your shoulders and learn from me, for I am gentle and humble of heart" (Mt. 11:29).

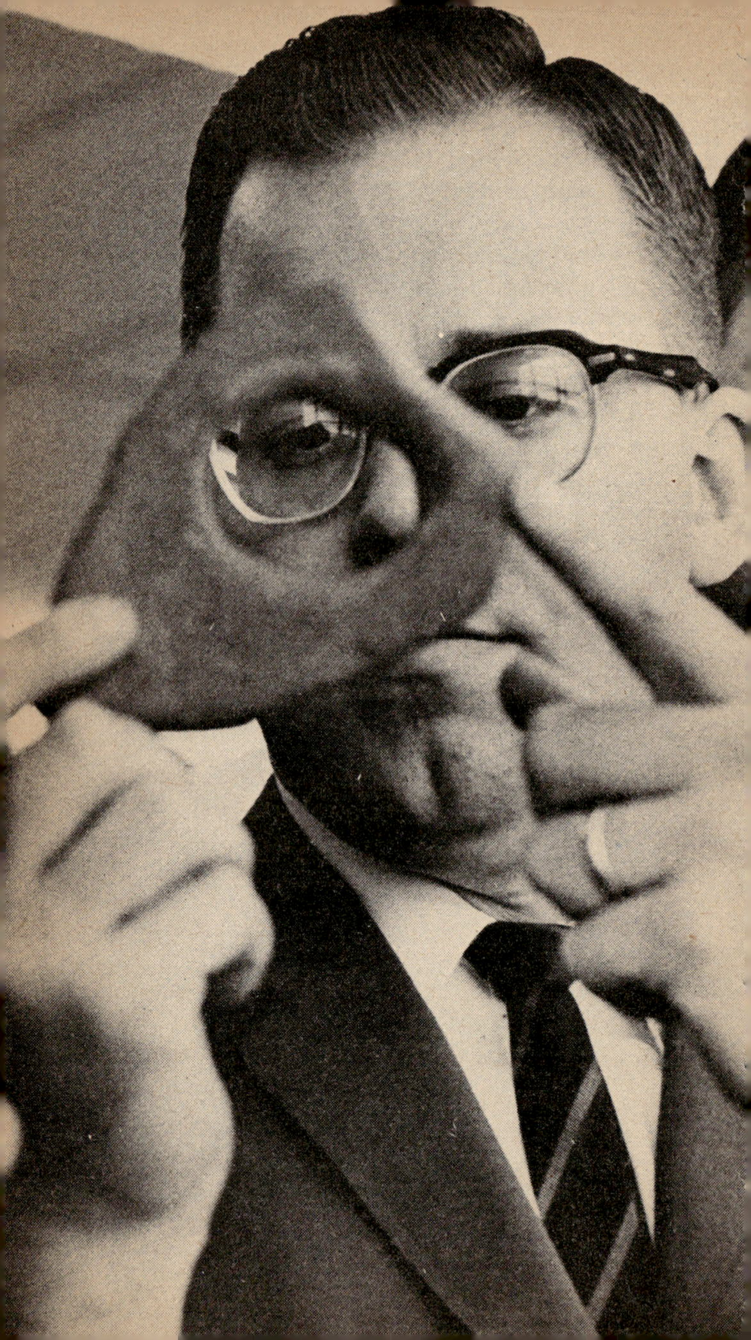

12. Maintaining Perspective

● Life is somewhat like a jig-saw puzzle. The puzzle, when it is in disarray, seems complex because one does not yet see how the pieces should fit together. When completed, however, the puzzle represents a simple, unified picture. So too with life. The purpose of life is really very simple — Jesus has told us to love God and neighbor with all our strength. Yet we can lose perspective concerning life's purpose for various reasons — and then our vision fails to see properly how the pieces of human existence should be appropriately arranged.

● Suffering, if we do not react to it with a Christian attitude, possesses a particularly powerful perspective-shattering force. Suffering can morbidly constrict the vision so that a person is aware of little else except his pain.

● The more closely we are united to Jesus, the more we are privileged to share his perfectly balanced view of human existence.

- Joy and happiness — intended by God to be strong catalysts for growth — can also be a heady wine. If we do not make attempts to share our joy with the Lord, it can create a sense of euphoria which makes us think too little of God, of duty and of other matters deserving our attention.

- When we begin to view our work as more ours than God's — what does this tell us?

- The burnt-out ashes of a part of life which was once cherished but now no longer exists can be the beginning of a wiser and more mature perspective.

- The healthy remembrance of death is a marvelously apt aid for maintaining perspective. We all are to die, and die soon — for even a hundred years is such a quickly passing span of time. Yet how often we misview persons, events, and circumstances precisely because we surrender to the illusion that this earthly sojourn will last forever.

- Straining after success in a non Spirit-inspired manner can make us miss so much of life's beauty and grandeur.

- The remembrance of how we have at times previously misjudged certain circumstances and events should make us somewhat cautious concerning the present. Not that we should be diffident individuals — but we should take those reasonable precautions which help assure proper judgments and decisions.

● A certain goal to be achieved or a certain event to be successfully encountered can loom so large in our consciousness that all of life seems to be gathered up and centered in this one point of time. Of course, the whole of life is obviously not so dependent on one such event. There will be many other important stops along the path of life — and we must remind ourselves of this.

● We must give ourselves as completely as possible to the present moment and the present task, but not in a manner which prevents a vision of transcendence, a vision which allows us properly to locate the present within the total drama of life.

● One of our greatest challenges in maintaining perspective is not to underestimate or overestimate our importance as individuals.

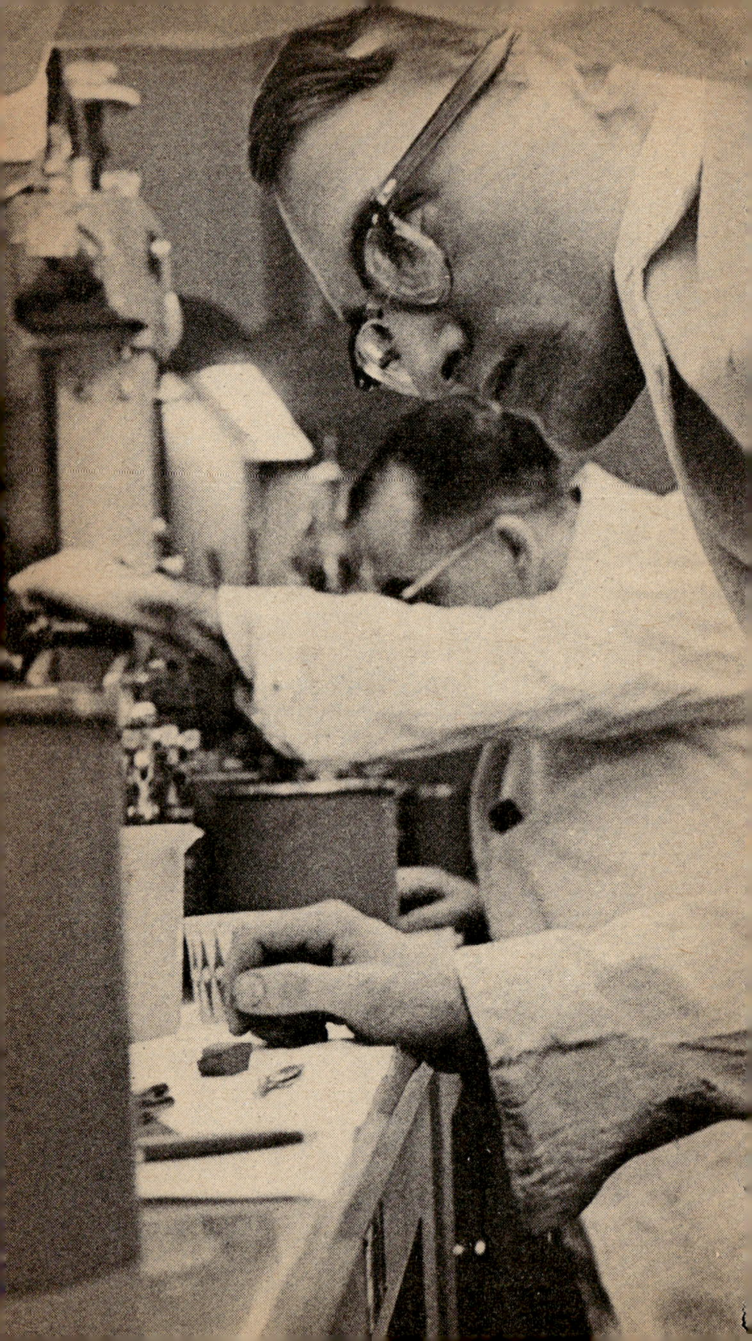

13. Inconsistencies

● At one moment of the day we can tell Jesus we are willing to make the greatest sacrifices for him. A bit later we fail him through the neglect of the most ordinary duties.

● A person can most vociferously condemn a certain fault in another, a fault of which he himself is much more guilty.

● A person can keep refusing the Spirit's call to a consistent prayer life proclaiming he is too busy, while consistently wasting time in frivolous activity.

● In the emergency room of a large hospital a medical team works with magnificent skill and dedication to save a life; in another part of the same hospital an abortion quickly terminates the life of a helpless victim.

- We can remain immersed in a painful situation because we fear the pain of the effort to extricate ourselves. Yet we really know that the former suffering is the greater.

- A person can devote a vastly disproportionate amount of time and energy to matters which are of such minor importance, yet he shows little or no concern for issues of great moment. To make matters worse, such a person is often oblivious of his inconsistency.

- When duties and commitments multiply to the point where time and energy seem insufficient to accomplish all, we long for the opportunity to rest, relax, and refurbish the spirit with leisurely reflection. And yet, when such a time does arrive, we can quickly develop a restlessness because we have not yet properly learned the secret of developing the more contemplative aspect of our human nature.

- In the depths of our heart we know that we need friendships and other personal encounters, and yet we can selfishly resist making our equitable contribution to these relationships.

14. On Being Relevant

● That which is relevant is appropriate or germane, fitting for the matter at hand. We see, then, that Jesus lived the perfectly relevant life, since he always did the perfectly appropriate thing according to his Father's good pleasure.

We see a paradox, then: many reject Jesus as being irrelevant and yet he is the supremely relevant one, for the relevancy of his life and message is perennial.

● Despite what others may think, when we act in accord with the Christic self, we are being relevant.

● Christian relevancy does indeed mean that we must strive to read the signs of the time and apply the Gospel message accordingly. In doing so, however, we must discern the difference between appropriate adaptation and false compromise. This is not always an easy task.

- Sometimes that which is most traditional is the most relevant; at other times, that which is most new. We must have the courage to choose accordingly.

- St. Paul had something to say about Christian relevancy: "Where is the wise man to be found? Where the scribe? Where is the master of worldly argument? Has not God turned the wisdom of this world into folly? Since in God's wisdom the world did not come to know him through 'wisdom,' it pleased God to save those who believe through the absurdity of the preaching of the gospel. Yes, Jews demand 'signs' and Greeks look for 'wisdom,' but we preach Christ crucified — a stumbling block to Jews, and an absurdity to Gentiles; but to those who are called, Jews and Greeks alike, Christ the power of God and the wisdom of God. For God's folly is wiser than men, and his weakness more powerful than men" (1 Cor. 1:20:25).

15. Reconciliation

● If there is any one characteristic that marks our present, it is cleavage, conflict, division, disharmony. This absence of unity, of oneness — ultimately of love — confronts us on four levels: between man and nature; within man himself; between man and man; between man and God."[1]

● "... if anyone is in Christ, he is a new creation. The old order has passed away; now all is new! All this has been done by God, who has reconciled us to himself through Christ and has given us the ministry of reconciliation. I mean that God, in Christ, was reconciling the world to himself, not counting men's transgressions against them, and that he has entrusted the message of reconciliation to us" (2 Cor. 5:17-19).

● A modern contradiction: contemporary man has achieved a startling mastery over the physical universe, yet in many ways he has increasingly alienated himself from the material world by misusing it.

- Modern man has a special need to come closer to his authentic self, to lay deeper hold on his real self-identity. It is strange, but true, that many apparently wander rather aimlessly through life without satisfactorily discovering their precious uniqueness.

We don't often think of reconciliation with ourselves — of the need to lessen the lack of harmony within, of the need to deepen contact with the true self — but such a need is always present in some degree.

- The bitter division which often exists between nations, between races, between citizens of the same community, even between members of the same family — this can be overwhelmingly discouraging unless we allow our sense of Christian optimism to remind us that, despite such a hideous display of man's evil, goodness still prevails. It is the task of each to promote this division-curing goodness of the human heart.

- "It pleased God to make absolute fullness reside in him and, by means of him, to reconcile everything in his person, both on earth and in the heavens, making peace through the blood of his cross.

"You yourselves were once alienated from him; you nourished hostility in your hearts because of your evil deeds. But now Christ has achieved reconciliation for you in his mortal body by dying, so as to present you to God holy, free of reproach and blame" (Col. 1:19:22).

- When a person contributes to the divisiveness among men, he deepens the divisiveness within himself.

- Proper contact with the beauty and grandeur of nature is a spirit-integrating experience.

- If I fail to nourish the union between myself and God, I simultaneously am failing to integrate further the various dimensions of my own being. For the closer I come to God, the more integrated, the more beautiful, the more wonderfully whole, becomes my entire self.

- There certainly is room for legitimate differences and criticism within the Christian community — for such in their own way ultimately contribute to a greater unity within the body. But the jealousies, enmities, hatreds, and displays of selfishness which rupture the community's unity and harmony constitute a tremendously ugly blemish on a people Jesus has called to be so intimately united by bonds of love.

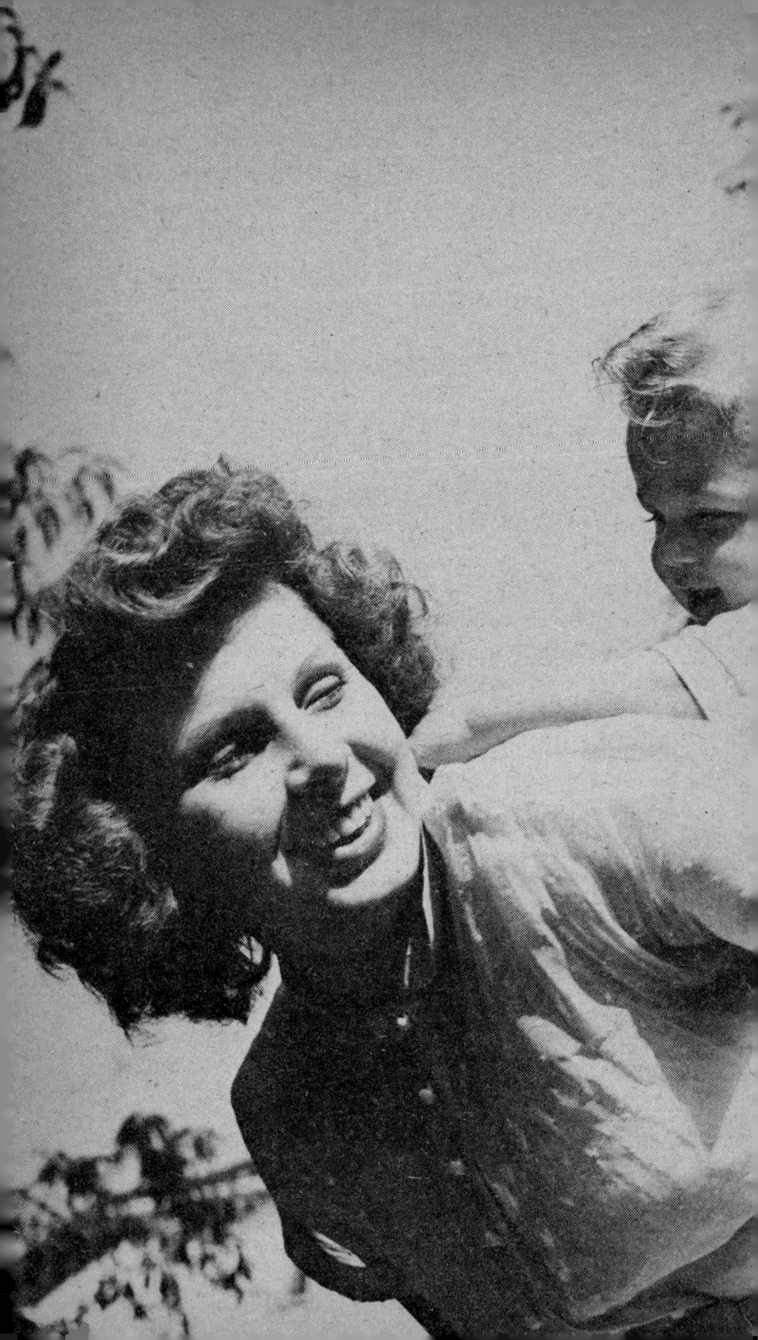

16. The Call To Be Joyful

● "Rejoice in the Lord always! I say it again. Rejoice! Everyone should see how unselfish you are. The Lord is near. Dismiss all anxiety from your minds. Present your needs to God in every form of prayer and in petitions full of gratitude. Then God's own peace, which is beyond all understanding, will stand guard over your hearts and minds, in Christ Jesus" (Phil. 4:4-7).

● Sorrow, suffering, anxieties of various sorts — these are all part of life within the human condition. Yet if we are not basically joyful people, something is remiss. The Christian vocation includes the call to be joyful. If we live properly in Christ Jesus, we will share his resurrection joy despite the painful dimension of being human.

● All this I tell you
that my joy may be yours
and your joy may be complete (Jn. 15:11).

- Western, industrialized culture has tended to create the illusion that joy can be bought, and that the more money one has, the greater the prospects of enjoying life. This tragic illusion has time and again prevented people from living in a manner which alone can give true joy.

- To place our joy too much in those things which are not necessary is necessarily to invite frustration.

- Real and lasting joy comes only when we are consistently willing to expend the effort required to live deep down at the center of our being.

- One of the greatest sources of joy is learning to share in the joy of others.

- To grasp life too tightly, feverishly seeking to extract all possible joys as often and as quickly as possible, is a sure path to frustration.

- "While we cannot in this life enjoy all that our Lord came on earth to give — we need a heaven in which to experience it — we can anticipate in faith what we cannot appreciate in fact. Is not this itself a joy?"[1]

- There are many daily occasions for experiencing joy, but we often pass them by unaware of their joy-producing possibilities because we have foolishly narrowed our expectations regarding what is a source of joy and what is not.

17. Escapism

● Christian prudence prompts us at times to avoid certain places, persons, things, and circumstances. To eliminate such confrontations as prompted by the Spirit's lead is obviously not a false flight from reality. But there is an avoidance of reality which is non-authentic, and we may term this escapism.

● Some flee from reality — the reality of their limitations — by attempting too much. Others, however, escape the demands of reality by attempting too little.

● It is not an uncommon form of escapism to look at the faults of others rather than our own, thus fleeing from the suffering required for self-improvement.

● There are numerous opportunities presented us each day for variously serving others. There are also numerous excuses we can conjure up for ignoring these occasions.

- If we dwell on the past and future to the neglect of the present, we are fleeing that time-span which alone we fully possess.

- If I work only half-heartedly at my present occupation, complaining that it is not worthy of my gifts, I am using a form of escapism which tells me I am lacking in the gift of humility.

- While constantly striving to develop my talents and correct my faults, I must simultaneously try to know the fundamental self God wants me to be. Otherwise, I am open to various non-authentic encounters with reality, and this is escapism: "For the human organism there is of course an inner, as well as an outer, reality... It is typical of the mature, well-adjusted individual that his actions be in reasonable accord with his inner reality."[1]

- Our modern culture provides an almost endless number of ways whereby we can escape solitude, a measure of which is necessary if we are to encounter our real selves in the presence of our God. And the more we flee our real selves, the more we flee authentic encounter with all dimensions of reality.

18. Seasons of Life

● Nature has its seasons ranging from springtime greenness to winter-time whiteness. Man also experiences different seasons — different life situations with a variety of human experiences.

● There is an appointed time for
  everything,
and a time for every affair under
  the heavens (Eccl. 3:1).

● The myriad experiences which God's providence maps out for us are varied opportunities for being and becoming Christian. Sometimes the growth process is very pleasant; at other times, very painful.

● Sometimes we have no choice whether a particular experience enters our lives. Our choice is rather how we will react to the occasion.

- There is a time when we wipe away the tears of others; there is also a time when we must realize how desperately we need to allow others to assuage our own sorrow.

- There are times when others acclaim us, praise our accomplishments, laud our talents. There are also times when people pass us by unnoticed, or ridicule us, or disdain us. Is it Christian to accept the former, but to become bitter concerning the latter?

- There is a time for basking in the glow of success, but also a time for courageously bearing the crush of failure. While enjoying the former, we must not allow success to become a heady wine; while enduring the latter, we must not permit failure's pain to give birth to a 'what's the use?" attitude.

- Sometimes we travel the path of life buoyed by enthusiasm, zeal, and confidence. At other times we trudge along hampered by lethargy, boredom, and diffidence.

- At times we grow by being with others; at times, by being alone.

- We are persons who are always the same and yet always different. We are persons with an unchangeable dimension and one which is always evolving. We are meant to experience the differentiated seasons of life being aware of both facets.

● There is a time for that which is old and a time for that which is new — but it is always the time to try to encounter each with all that we are proportionate to the occasion.

● There is a time for work and a time for enjoying the fruits of one's labor. There is a time for laughter and a time for tears, for helping others and being helped by them, for receiving love but also enduring the pain of rejection, for understanding why things happen and for bearing with the pain of unknowing. Yes, there is a time for these and other human experiences, but especially is there a time for love. As Christians, we are called to love and love deeply all day, every day, allowing love to charge with vitality all that we are and all that we do, allowing love to gather up the rich variety of human experiences into a marvelous, Christic unity.

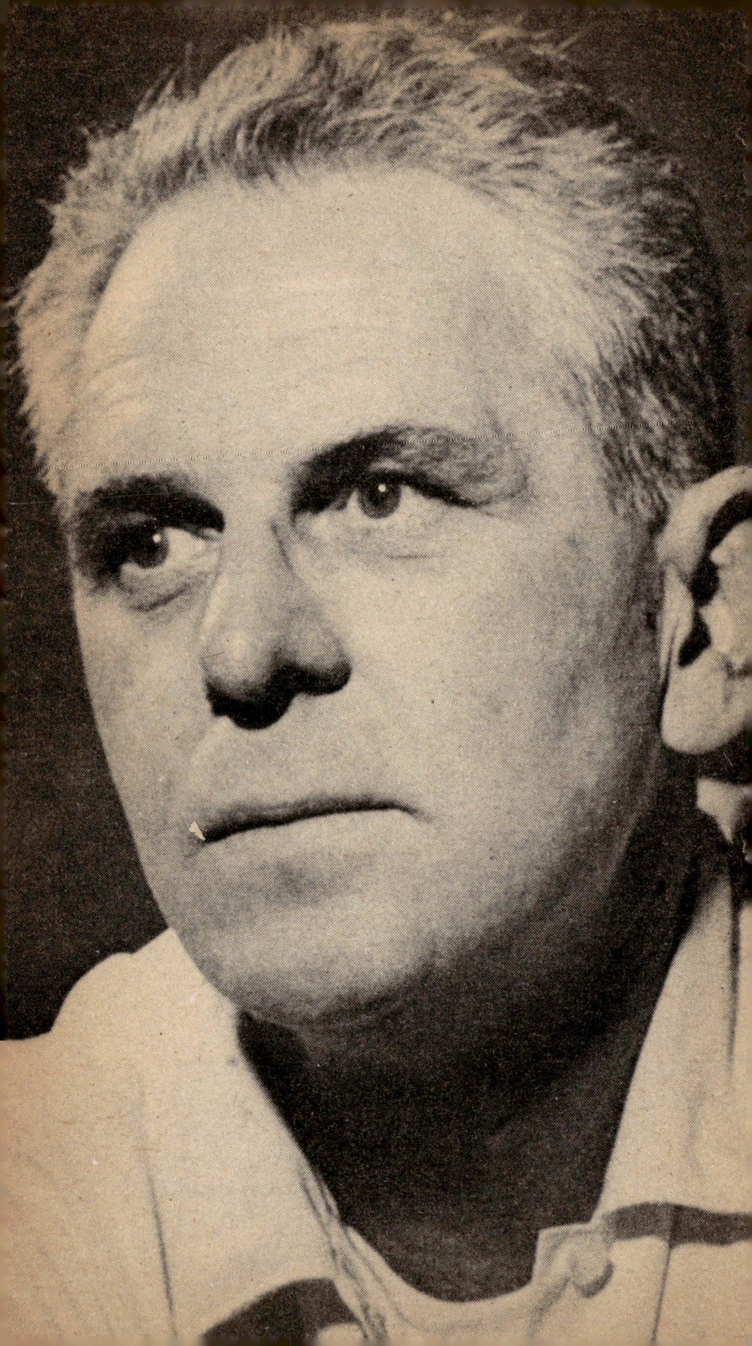

19. The Role of Patience

- Accept whatever befalls you,
  in crushing misfortune be patient... (Sir. 2:4).

- At times we are guilty of running ahead of God, wanting things to be accomplished more quickly than his will allows.

- We can be an enigma to ourselves — at one time we are impatiently overeager in wanting to accomplish a certain something, while at other times we procrastinate with all sorts of silly excuses regarding that same something.

- At times we can prudently avoid others who try our patience. However, there is no such escape from the self — and sometimes bearing with ourselves draws upon the deepest reservoirs of our patience.

The Jesus Experience

● Some eagerly join great causes, and their admirable talents promise that they will contribute magnificently to the effort. However, eventually they withdraw from the struggle because patient endurance was not theirs in sufficient degree.

● Which is the greater patience — that required properly to encounter the constant trials of everydayness, or that required for the proper acceptance of a rather brief but agonizing crisis?

● The development of some is hindered not so much because they themselves lack patience, but because others, such as parents and educators, lack the patience required to help them grow properly.

● We can vacillate between an impatient desire to cure the Church's and world's ills overnight, and a lackadaisical attitude which contributes little or nothing to the improvement of things. Maintaining an attitude which avoids both extremes is no easy challenge.

● At certain critical stages along life's journey, we seek mightily to know God's will for us. There are certain signs which point in this direction, others which point in that. It is not yet clear what God would have us do. Suffering ensues, but the degree of the pain must be matched by our patient endurance as we pray for the light to recognize which choice the Spirit would have us make.

20. Limitations

● There are many things we would like to do and accomplish in life, yet we realize that to choose the pursuit of certain accomplishments means we must abandon the hope of achieving others. This fact points to our creaturehood. The very fact that we are creatures of God means that we are limited beings, restricted in various ways by our finitude. Only God is without limitations. This is what we mean by saying he is infinite. Serenely to accept our status of being limited creatures, while at the same time striving to develop our talents to the fullest, is a significant sign of Christian maturity.

● There comes a time in our lives when certain motives, which mightily spurred us on in earlier years, have become burnt out. We can become hemmed in, therefore, within very narrow confines of accomplishment — unless we develop new motives, or properly recondition the old ones to meet the present challenge.

● Another false set of limitations arises when we glide along the surface of life burdened with a terrible mediocrity, failing, for one reason or the other, to grasp the fullness of each day by living life at its deep center where the really real is dynamically encountered.

● Certain things are more appropriately and effectively engaged in by the young, other things, more so by those advanced in years. This is an obvious truth — yet both groups can be stubbornly blind of the fact in actual practice.

● We can impose a false type of limitation upon ourselves — by striving to do that which we are ill-equipped to accomplish while neglecting those tasks God has admirably gifted us to undertake and complete.

● Sometimes we become overanxious and devoid of peace because we are trying to accomplish too much, or because we are going about it in the wrong way, or, even, because we are trying to accomplish that which God does not intend for us.

● The sense of my personal limitations can be lessened by rejoicing in the accomplishments of others. After all, we are all serving the same Lord for the same purpose. What we cannot be and accomplish, another can. We are one body in Christ: There are different gifts but the same Spirit; there are different ministries but the same Lord; there are different works but the same God who accomplishes all of them. (1 Cor. 12:4-7).

21. The Power of Affirmation

● God has created and redeemed us. All are precious in his sight. Why don't we more often affirm this preciousness and dignity inherent in each individual?

● It seems strange that we often wait until a person dies to give him or her due praise.

● Could it be that we are somewhat jealous of others' gifts if we rarely offer praise and affirmation?

● Just one act of affirming another can help change the course of that person's life.

● We can play a waiting game, proclaiming that our main opportunity to accomplish good has not yet arrived. Yet all the while we can waste countless opportunities of helping others — such as variously letting them know that we think they are worthwhile persons with more to offer.

- Some require more affirmation than others, but we all need some.

- Jesus gave attention to individuals whom the world often passes by — those burdened with derision, the lame, and the sick.

- A person obviously has to be appropriately corrected at times. Yet proper words of affirmation are much more efficacious in aiding a person to grow than are words of correction.

- Words are not the only form of affirmation — a touch, a smile, a look, a tone of voice can also convey the message.

22. Contemplative Awareness

● The contemplative attitude or spirit is operative not only during times of formal prayer. It is also keenly alive during the myriad experiences of everydayness. It sees how all creation mirrors forth the goodness, the truth, and the beauty of God himself, and how this creation is thrust toward God.

● "Our culture is hungry for completely 'people-oriented' individuals who refuse to let their spontaneity be suppressed by the performance principle. Our culture is hungry for those people who feel it is enough just to *be* a person; to be defined simply by their relationship to God and to other people. We believe that this is the distinguishing characteristic of the true contemplative' way of life."[1]

● Strange as it may seem to some, the contemplative is very efficient. He is consistently aware of the necessity of listening to the Spirit and following his lead. Is there a more efficient way of life?

● Many look upon contemplation as being rather useless and impractical. Yet what the world desperately needs is more individuals immersed in the contemplative spirit. The contemplative is one who is deeply in touch wtih the really real, one who is eminently capable of helping mankind learn what it means to be human. The contemplative, then, is one who is extremely practical — for what could be more practical than knowing how to live human existence to the fullest?

We can mcander through life often guided by a relatively superficial awareness, failing to develop a Christian consciousness which permits us to live with an ever-growing dynamism.

To live the really real does not mean doing altogether different things than we are presently doing. It means rather that we do basically the same things differently — that we go about our days living at a deeper level.

We must constantly strive to penetrate to the inner and true reality of things, not being satisfied with a surface vision. We must seek to see all more according to the vision of Jesus and react accordingly.

● The contemplative is very love conscious. He sees much more love existing in the world than does the average person. On the other hand, he is also more conscious of how much the world desperately needs an increase of love.

● The contemplative is very much in touch with himself and others — because he is very much in touch with God.

● Being human, the contemplative is not immune from feelings of boredom and lethargy. Yet, because he is intensely in touch with the really real, he is keenly aware that a new beauty and freshness impregnates each succeeding day.

● The contemplative can be deeply moved by an experience which seems so prosaic to others.

● The contemplative is not critical of activity — only of that activity which is not God-oriented.

● If one is properly aware of his true self and is loyal to this consciousness, then he will experience a basic peace which even the deepest suffering cannot destroy.

● We can fail to actuate the rich potential of the present moment because our contemplative awareness of its preciousness is dulled by our thoughts dwelling too much on the past or future.

● Although there are many advantages of a technological and industrialized society, it creates an atmosphere which can seriously hamper our contemplative awareness. We must take appropriate means that such a tragedy does not occur.

● To be so aware of ourselves that we hardly think of others is indeed to be afflicted by a morbid consciousness.

● A vital awareness of each individual's priceless dignity is a precious gift of the Spirit.

- Being aware of the grandeur of God's creation is a daily opportunity, yet how often we can be blind to the beauty which surrounds us.

- A contemplative awareness that our doing is an expression of our being is extremely important, yet a consciousness not easily achieved. We can be so taken up with doing that we fail properly to develop our being, and to this extent our doing is burdened with a horrendous mediocrity.

- To be aware how much Jesus loves us and to respond accordingly — this is the key to happiness.

23. Touches of Goodness

● The news media consistently tells us about the evil in the world, seldom about its goodness. But amid all the evil, the goodness is there in plentiful measure — if we are sensitive enough to discern.

● A man was seated on a bus with a bouquet of flowers in his lap. The young girl next to him kept glancing at the flowers, admiring their attractiveness. As the man rose to leave, he said to the girl, "I bought these for my wife, but, here, you take them. I don't think my wife would mind." The startled girl said thank you and watched her kind benefactor as he walked away from the bus. She noticed he was heading for a gate with two stone pillars supporting overhead an arch spelling out the words, "Cemetery."

● A stranger passes us, smiles and says hello — and this makes a difference.

- At times we can become increasingly pessimistic concerning the evil and selfishness which seem to pervade so much of the modern world. Then we read or hear about people's overwhelmingly generous response to help those in a disaster area, or to aid a family stricken with a sudden and devastating tragedy. Our spirits are renewed, and our trust in the goodness of human hearts is refurbished, and we are motivated to develop further our own concern and care for others.

- Penetrating through to the priceless dignity of each individual and reacting accordingly is a constant opportunity for exercising goodness.

- The almost unnoticed but consistent acts of goodness displayed by ordinary people the world over does more to hold together the human family than do the more publicized acts of statesmen and other leaders.

- The uninhibited innocence of little children, manifested in so many ways, can be a reminder to us that we must work at eradicating the blemishes disfiguring that goodness God has instilled in each of us — but which we have over the years betrayed more times than we like to admit.

- A certain disc-jockey closes out his program by saying, "Be especially nice to somebody today." We should ask ourselves whether such an idea is important to us, and if not, why not.

● "He glanced up and saw the rich putting their offerings into the treasury, and also a poor widow putting in two copper coins. At that he said: 'I assure you, this poor widow has put in more than all the rest. They make contributions out of their surplus, but she from her want has given what she could not afford — every penny she had to live on'" (Lk. 21:1-4).

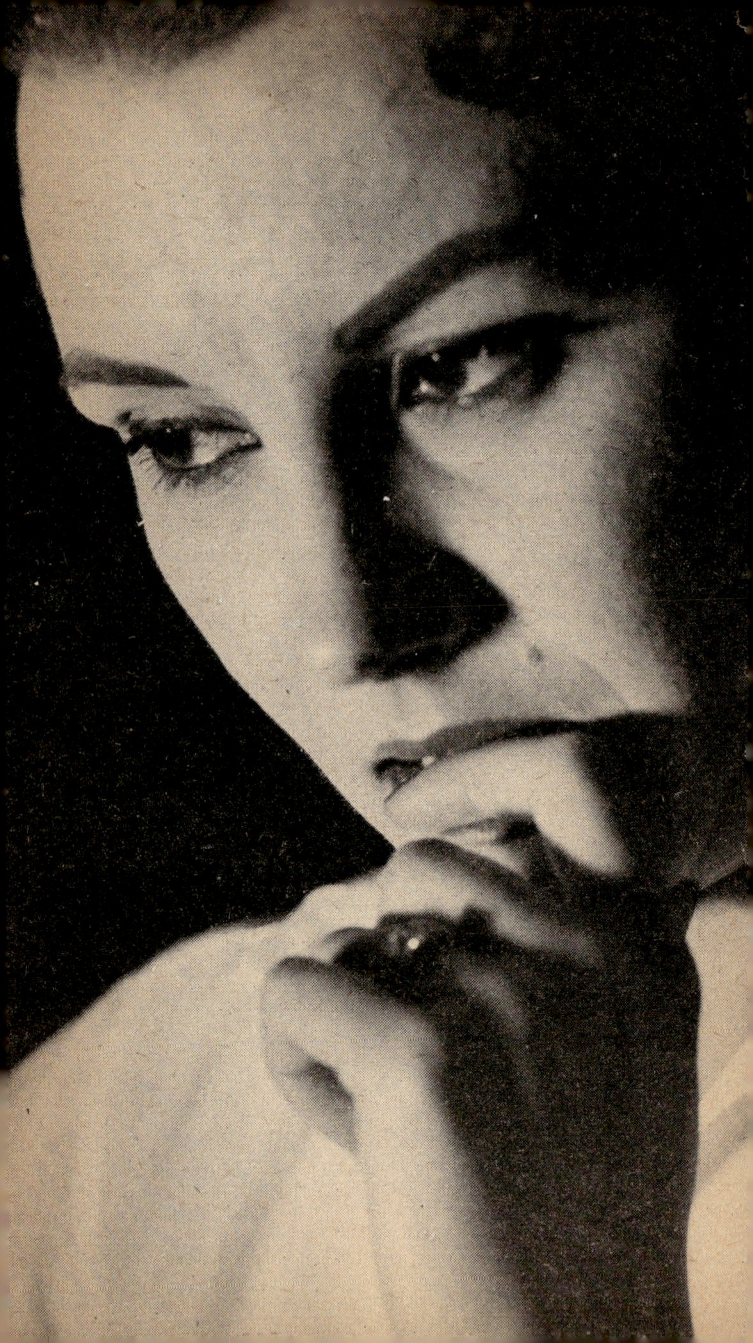

24. Memories

● At certain times in life we experience the Lord's presence in a very special manner. Later on, during periods of special difficulty, we remember these occasions, and we are encouraged to struggle on.

● We can recall the deep sufferings of yesterday with a certain joy — if we have become better persons through proper encounter with the pain.

● We remember, with a wonder at the mystery involved, the meetings with certain special people along the path of life. Without them we realize that we most probably would not have grown in certain dimensions of our being — that without them our becoming would have been somewhat impoverished.

● We remember those occasions when we failed to be kind and loving and gentle. The recall of missed opportunities in the past should motivate us to be more faithful in the future.

- Very special moments with very special persons — such memories remain etched deep within our being. Whether such memories now occasion feelings of sadness or joy, we know that these experiences have made us Christians of greater depth — and for this we can rejoice.

- If the recall of certain experiences fills us with bitterness, we should realize that this portion of our memories requires the healing touch of Jesus.

- We look back on those occasions which demanded a heroic response. What was asked of us seemed so disproportionate to our talents, our degree of spiritual development, or our psychological state. And yet respond we did, and we weathered the storm. Then we realized, as we do now in reminiscing, that the strength of the Lord carried us. Such a realization is an occasion both of renewed gratitude to the Lord and of consolation emanating from the knowledge that at any future date we can do all things in him who strengthens us.

25. *The Thrust of Hope*

● The realization of how weak and helpless we are without Jesus is a thought which is meant to fill us with joy — such a thought is an opportunity for renewing our trust in the Lord and for once again abandoning ourselves to his love, and concern, and strength: "Therefore I am content with weakness, with mistreatment, with distress, with persecutions and difficulties for the sake of Christ; for when I am powerless, it is then that I am strong" (2 Cor. 12:10).

● If our days are too much colored with discouragement and pessimism, our sense of hope has become dormant. We must rekindle it and tell ourselves that we belong to Jesus and that nothing, absolutely nothing, should destroy the basic peace and joy he desires for us.

● How fortunate for the Christian that his faith vision and hope thrust can carry him beyond the toil, the pain, and the anxiety of the present moment.

- 'Eye has not seen, ear has not heard,
nor has it so much as dawned on
  man
what God has prepared for those
  who love him' (1 Cor. 2:9).

- In times of distress we instinctively turn to Jesus, immediately realizing the need for trust. However, we do not so easily realize our need for him during times when all goes smoothly and a sense of joy seems to touch every fibre of our being. Yet we also need to be cognizant of our dependence on Jesus during these happy episodes. For if during times of distress we need to trust in the Lord for patient endurance, during times of joy we are in no less need of his help. We need his light and strength to use these periods not selfishly or greedily, but as he wills.

- Is there any great cause which has not demanded from its proponents great measures of hope? No less is demanded of us Christians as we contribute to the greatest cause of all — that of the Lord Jesus Christ.

- "For I am certain that neither death nor life, neither angels nor principalities, neither the present nor the future, nor powers, neither height nor depth nor any other creature, will be able to separate us from the love of God that comes to us in Christ Jesus, our Lord" (Rom. 8:38).

26. Searching

● O God, you are my God whom I
  seek;
for you my flesh pines and my soul
  thirsts
like the earth, parched, lifeless and
  without water (Ps. 63:2).

● The search for God is a continuing quest. It is not that we do not already possess him through his graciousness. It is rather that he wants us to thirst for a deeper love union with him — until eternal life quenches our thirst completely. Then our hearts will be brim-full and overflowing, overflowing with the loveliness of our God.

● The on-going search for God is simultaneously an on-going search for myself. The more I find God, the more I discover my Christic divinized self — and this is the real self.

● It should scare us if we stop thirsting for God.

- We can seek happiness in all sorts of ways — through persons, places, things, and varied activity. But if we do not simultaneously seek God — do not try to relate to all else according to his will — then the quest of these other things will leave a bitter taste, and we will complain that life is full of illusions, of things that promise fulfillment but contain only frustrated emptiness.

- The continuing search for God involves the continuing search for our neighbor. This is such an obvious truth of the Gospel, yet it is also an obvious fact that we can easily forget this fundamental maxim.

- There's a mood that can come upon us — we feel terribly uneasy with our present terrible mediocrity, a state that has made God seem far away. This is a precious moment — if we respond to the challenge and once more intensely seek the lovely face of God.

27. *Eucharist*

● "Let us imagine that the priest is about to offer the host at the altar, and that this host is made from bread which during the week *we* earned and kneaded ourselves. What kind of bread is the priest going to consecrate?... How terrible it would be if we offered to God, for him to become incarnate in, a bread of hate, bitterness, rancor, disgust. Will it be the bread of justice and honesty, a bread of love of our brothers, a bread joyfully kneaded in respect for the mission which has been entrusted to us?" [1]

● The Eucharist is narrative. Through the Scriptural readings we hear the greatest love story of all time — God's love story.

● The Eucharist is covenant. We offer as a religious community, as the people of God, not as isolated individuals. How incongruous, then, if we do not do all in our power to eliminate from our hearts attitudes of divisiveness.

- The Eucharist is ethic. In receiving the Eucharistic Christ we are pledging ourselves to live as he did. We are to continuously die and rise with him. As he did before us, so must we live the painful, harsh, and sometimes bitter dimension of human existence in order to achieve greater life for ourselves and others.

- The Eucharist as meal, offering us the one and same Christ, is a sign and cause, not only of our union with Jesus, but also with one another.

- The Eucharist is celebration. It is a calling to mind of the Christ event. It is a re-enactment of that event. As with all celebrations, the Eucharist should remind us that a special occasion is at hand, yet with a warmth and congeniality that makes one want to be present for the festivity.

- The Eucharist is sacrifice or offering. We offer ourselves with Jesus to the Father under the Spirit's action. We offer both what has already transpired and that which is yet to come. We offer our entire lives as guided by the Father's will. We offer in love — a response to his constant and mighty and tender love. We tell the Father to take all of our lives — the laughter and the tears, the work and the play, the joy and the suffering. We tell him as he has given all to us, we wish to return all to him.

28. Experiencing God

● Sometimes when God seems so distant, so difficult to encounter, he is, in actuality, more present than ever.

● To experience God is to experience all else with greater meaning.

● "Thus, the Eastern Fathers developed the highest type of contemplation in terms of an apophatic theology. Apophatic is usually translated as negative, but this is to misunderstand the nuanced mysticism of these early Fathers. The accent is entirely on God doing the revealing, giving the Gift of Himself.... God who is so infinitely perfect and good, the incomprehensible, deigns to allow us to know Him in some fashion or other by way of a direct experience."[1]

● Why do we so eagerly seek out God in times of suffering, yet often easily relegate him to the peripheries of consciousness in times of joy?

- To seek the full sweetness of life without God is eventually to taste empty bitterness

- Jesus can vividly manifest himself in times and circumstances that, to us, indicated beforehand no special encounter with the Lord.

- The Spirit sometimes whispers his desires very softly; at other times he manifests his will with the force of a mighty wind.

- Christian spirituality begins with the experience of God in Christ Jesus, and until there is real encounter with Christ, until he is a person to us and we are persons to him, we are still on the level of Old Testament religion, the religion of law and ritual. Creeds and codes and rituals have their place. But they are preambles or corollaries, conceptualizations and theologizing about the Christian fact rather than the life itself."[2]

- There is an encounter with the Lord permeated with sweetness and consolation; there is another filled with darkness and desolation. To desire the former and eschew the latter is to seek ourselves rather than God.

- Laughter and tears, success and failure, acclaim and ridicule, work and play, joy and sorrow — the sensitive spirit will recognize that these varied human experiences are simultaneously opportunities for variously encountering the Lord.

● Some are called to seek the face of Jesus in the dust of the market place; a very few are inspired by the Spirit to encounter him surrounded by the awful stillness of the desert sands.

● We have such a persistent tendency to want to experience God in all sorts of ways except the way which is the opportunity of the present moment.

● Do we prefer to experience God among throngs of people or in solitude? As a social worker amid the explosive anguish of the inner city or as a research scientist surrounded by the walls of academe? As married or as celibate? Really, the only authentic preference regarding these and all other possibilities is the preference of God himself — something we at times are reluctant to consider.

● At times we experience God through the proper use of something; at other times, through the renunciation of that same something.

● How to seek the presence of the Holy One both within ourselves and without — this is our challenge.

● "When from the sublime words of the Lord resembling the summit of a mountain I looked down into the ineffable depths of His thoughts, my mind had the experience of a man who gazes from a high ridge into the immense sea below him." [3]

- How quickly one's tears can be banished by the tender touch of Jesus.

- When we abandon the presence of God, we simultaneously abandon the presence of our authentic selves.

- One's historical and cultural situation condition one's experience of the Lord.

- We must be willing to undergo the on-going purification of mystical death in order to experience with increasing intensity the transforming love of God.

- It should be a frightening experience not to want to experience the Lord.

- "We have said that the religious experience is a grasp, in all that is human and terrestrial, of the import of the Other. This Other is the prop of existence, the horizon of the true reality to which the passing phenomena of life should be referred, the absolute owner of all human existence. Present and distant, pervading significant objects without coinciding with them; that is what is meant by the antithesis of the sacred and the profane which is the only way religion can be characterized." [4]

- Meaningful liturgy is a great source of religious experience. But we can hardly expect to find meaningful liturgy if we ourselves are not meaningful Christians.

- Only in God is my soul at rest;
    from him comes my salvation.
  He only is my rock and my
      salvation,
      my stronghold; I shall not be
        disturbed at all   (Ps. 62:2-3).

- The Lord awaits us in the pages of Scripture. If this magnificent book is for us often a closed book, we should with considerable concern ask ourselves why.

- The vital realization of how much Jesus loves me — this is the foundation of the Christian experience.

FOOTNOTES

1. Karl Rahner, **Theological Investigations,** Vol. 1 (Baltimore: Helicon, 1965), p. 199.
2. Andrew Greeley, **The Jesus Myth** (New York: Doubleday, 1971), p. 37.
3. Luigi Santucci, **Meeting Jesus** (New York: Herder and Herder, 1971), p. 46.
4. Thomas Merton, **A Thomas Merton Reader** (New York: Doubleday Image Books, 1974), p. 371.
5. Saint Augustine, **Sermons on the Liturgical Seasons** as in **The Fathers of the Church,** Vol. 38 (New York: Fathers of the Church, Inc.), pp. 42-43.
6. St. Ignatius of Antioch, **The Letters** as in **The Fathers of the Church,** Vol. 1, op. cit., p. 110.

1. Michael Lawrence, C.SS.P., "You Have to Love to Teach," Ligourian, September, 1974, p. 4.
2. Thomas Merton, **Contemplative Prayer** (New York: Doubleday (Image), 1971), p. 75.

1. Hubert Van Zeller, **Considerations** (Springfield: Templegate, 1973), p. 37.
2. Bernard Haring, **Christian Maturity** (New York: Herder and Herder, 1967), p. 50.

1. Vatican II, **Decree on the Apostolate of the Laity,** No. 5. as in **The Teachings of the Second Vatican Council** (Westminster: Newman Press, 1966).

1. Henri Nouwen, **The Wounded Healer** (New York: Doubleday, 1972), p. 86.

1. John Donne, "Devotions upon Emergent Occasions," XVII, as in **John Donne, Complete Poetry and Selected Prose,** edited by John Hayward (London: The Nonesuch Press, 1962), p. 538.
2. Ladislas Orsy, "On Being One with the Church Today," in **Studies in the Spirituality of Jesuits,** Vol. VII, January, 1975.
3. Avery Dulles, **Models of the Church** (New York: Doubleday, 1974), p. 63.
4. Karl Rahner, **Theological Investigations,** Vol. IX (New York: Herder and Herder, 1972), p. 188.

1. Thomas Oden, **The Structure of Awareness** (New York: Abingdon Press, 1969), pp. 23-24.

2. Henri Nouwen, **Reaching Out** (New York: Doubleday, 1975), p. 82.

1. Joseph Blenkinsopp, "We Rejoice in Our Sufferings" in **The Mystery of Suffering and Death,** edited by Michael Taylor (New York: Doubleday, 1974), p. 72.

1. Karl Rahner, **On Prayer** (New York: Paulist Press, 1968), pp. 54-55.

2. St. John of the Cross, **The Dark Night,** Ch. 9, in **The Collected Works of St. John of the Cross,** translated by Kieran Kavanaugh, O.C.D., and Otilio Rodriguez (New York: Doubleday, 1964), p. 346.

3. Karl Rahner, **Encounters with Silence** (New York: Paulist-Newman Press, 1960), p. 21.

1. Walter Burghardt, **Towards Reconciliation** (Washington: United States Catholic Conference, 1974), pp. 1-2.

1. Hubert Van Zeller, **Considerations** (Springfield: Templegate, 1973), p. 34.

1. Charles Hofling, M.D., **Textbook of Psychiatry for Medical Practice,** Second Edition (Philadelphia: J. B. Lippincott Company, 1968), p. 36.

1. Gerard Fourez, **A Light Grasp on Life** (Dimension Books: Denville, 1975), p. 38.

1. Louis Evely, **Joy** (New York: Doubleday, 1974), pp. 63-64.

1. George Maloney, S.J., **The Breath of the Mystic** (Denville: Dimension Books, 1974), p. 72.

2. Ernest Larkin, "The Search for Experience" in **The Way,** Vol. II (1971), p. 101.

3. St. Gregory of Nyssa, **The Lord's Prayer and the Beatitudes** as in **Ancient Christian Writers,** Vol. 18 (Westminster: Newman Press, 1954), p. 143.

4. Antoine Vergote, **The Religious Man** (Dayton: Pflaum Press, 1969), p. 42.

ALBA BOOKS
DIV. OF SOC. OF ST. PAUL · CANFIELD OHIO 44406

103 — RESPONSE IN CHRIST — A Study of the Christian Life 1.45 ppr

A masterful blend of current-day spirituality and the authentic, essential and unchanging elements which have constantly inserted themselves throughout the history of Christian spirituality.

109 — THE SPIRIT IS PRESENT
by Edward Carter 1.25 ppr
Hard cover edition 5.95

Christian spirituality concerns itself with our total human life lived in Christ under the guidance of the Spirit. We can, then, immediately see one of the root meanings of the terms spirituality and spiritual life.

121 — NOW IS THE TIME
by Edward Carter, S.J. 1.45 ppr.

A "prayer starter," an aid to personal meditation, based on the Bible. Useful to groups engaged in shared prayer. An inspiration to happiness and optimism.

113 — JESUS, I WANT TO TALK WITH YOU
by Edward Carter, S.J.   4.95

Whether we work, or pray, or love one another, or feel joy or pain — all these and other aspects of our daily life are of interest to Jesus. He wants us to talk to Him about them. The language of these prayers is intimate, familiar, informal.

This book has a mass audience appeal — for both Catholics and Protestants. For all kinds of people, including those who would like to pray but don't know how.

BODY OF CHRIST by Earnest Larsen, C.SS.R. — Splendid, modern reflections, enriched by apt illustrations, on the everyday reality of the Eucharistic Sacrament which is inseparably linked to the flesh and blood Sacrifice of Calvary and which the author with great sensitivity leads us to find as surely in the tenement as in the Tabernacle.

— $1.75

THE ROSARY: A Gospel Prayer by Wilfrid J. Harrington, O.P. — We tend to think of the Rosary as the great Marian prayer but in fact it is largely concerned with Mary's Son. Fr. Harrington, the noted Scripture scholar in clear and simple language here illustrates the firm Gospel basis of the Rosary and offers proof that the Rosary, far from being a relic of the past, is in fact more worthwhile than ever.

— $1.65

THE HOUR OF THE HOLY SPIRIT by Serafino Falvo — The Charismatic Movement continues to spread. This book is a revelation: testimony piles on testimony of the radical changes people have experienced in their lives. It is an excellent presentation of the Charismatic Movement and will encourage many to go deeper into the life of the Spirit.

— $3.30

Are there ALBA BOOKS titles you want but cannot find in your local stores? Simply send name of book and retail price plus 30¢ to cover mailing and handling costs to:
ALBA BOOKS, Canfield, Ohio, 44406.